THE UN

OUTLANDER BOOK OF HERBS

M. McIntosh

SASSENACH PRESS

SASSENACH PRESS

The Unofficial Outlander Book of Herbs

M. McIntosh

Editor: Deborah Aubrey-Peyron

Cover Design and Interior Artwork: Kerry Robinson at Kerry Illustrator

Interior Design: Steve Shetter Jr.

Information on the plants mentioned in the Outlander book series came from http://outlanderlists.weebly.com/ along with books listed below.

Outlander by Diana Gabaldon. New York, NY : Bantam Dell, 1992
Cross Stitch by Diana Gabaldon. London : Arrow Books, 1994
Dragonfly in Amber by Diana Gabaldon. London : Arrow Books, 1992
Voyager by Diana Gabaldon. London : Arrow Books, 1994
The Exile : an Outlander graphic novel / by Diana Gabaldon, illustrated by Hoang Nguyen. New York : Ballantine Books, 2010
A Trail of Fire : four Outlander tales by Diana Gabaldon. London : Orion Books, 2012
Virgins by Diana Gabaldon. In **Dangerous Women** / edited by George R.R. Martin and Gardner Dozois. New York : Tor, 2013
The Outlandish Companion by Diana Gabaldon. New York, NY :

Delacorte Press, 1999
The Outlandish Companion : volume two by Diana Gabaldon.
London : Century, 2015

Published in the United States by Sassenach Press

ISBN 9781973233848

To my loving Sassenach, Claire Elizabeth Fraser
From Jamie Alexander Malcolm MacKenzie Fraser
March 20, 1746

CONTENTS

DISCLAIMER:

In honor of timeless stories of sacrifice for true loves, I imaged this book as a support for Claire's hobby that she explored during WWII and continued after the war. While Frank would see her looking at and reading books on botany, Jamie only assumed that Claire's interest was strictly as a healer. Later on in their marriage, Jamie gave Claire a book by which she could record information about the plants and collect specimens during their travels. No this is not a field guide nor a botany book. It is also not a gardening book by strict definition. Instead, this book combines ethnobotany based on the Outlander book series and STARZ show along with gardening techniques for each herb mentioned in Outlander (Cross Stitch), Dragonfly in Amber, and Voyager.

As you may have noticed by the list of herbs, some of these plants are not herbs by pure definition. In this context, any plant used to treat humans is referred to as an herb.

While the book cover/design may be a little unmemorable and untidy, the goal was to make this book look like a book from the 1740s, which was loved, shared and carried. The tattering along the edges as the story goes, came from the rubbing of Claire's saddlebag along with the shifting around in her medical kit. The red circle on the book cover is to resemble an old wax seal. In a sense, sealing up the sacred and mysterious knowledge that healers like Master Raymond and Claire had learned. A knowledge that was only available to a few.

The most touching part of this book's back story comes from the signed page. Growing up as child, I had an aunt that always gave me a book for my birthday. As part of the gift, she would write who the book was to, who it was from, and the date. This was a very special touch and I wanted to include this in the book. Yes, Jamie and Claire are fictional characters in a wonderful fictional story by Diana Gabaldon but there true love is eternal. I never image Jamie giving Claire a book without signing it, preserving their true love for the ages.

After Claire had gone back through the stones and Jamie started the print shop, he began printing this book as a way of remembering Claire.

While the background for this book is fictional and not part of the Outlander series, I am also not associated with the Outlander book series, STARZ show and/or Diana Gabaldon. Whereas I am an expert in the field of Agriculture, I do not support wilding and/or making your own medicine from herbs. If you have this interest, seek out a professional by which you can safely learn this skill.

PREFACE

The sound of my great-grandmother's laughter echoed through her house as I entered through her heavy front door. She was clothed as she always was-- in a dress, flower printed apron, and ankle boots. We sat in her parlor for awhile as she played with my hair, but then I saw that oh-so- familiar twinkle in her eye. I knew what this meant. It meant she had something new in the garden to show me. As if it was magic, before I knew it we were off the couch going through her dining room, kitchen, and finally into the mudroom. Once we were through the mudroom, we entered my great grandmother's magical world of plants or what I would call her enchanted garden.

Before I move on with this story, let me explain something about my great-grandmother. She did not have a high school diploma but was an expert on botany and horticulture. Her front yard never gave a hint as to what was behind her house. It was very proper for the time and consisted of grass with perfectly manicured shrubs that hugged the front porch. To add color to the space, she had two large concrete planters that framed the interior of the portico. These simple-looking containers were brought to life every summer with marigolds, begonias, and snapdragons.

Another interesting detail about my great-grandmother's life was the fact that she traveled across the plains with her family in a Conestoga wagon. Since there was not much to do as she walked along the wagon, she would collect twigs, pick flowers, and gather interesting seedpods. This was truly the beginning of her enchanted garden and the sprouts of curiosity that it took to learn all she could about botany and horticulture.

As my great-grandmother grabbed my hand as we walked through the mudroom, I could feel the sweat of anticipation coming through her hand. Keep in mind, my great-grandmother was only 4 ft. 5 in. in height. But her excitement for the natural world made her seem to me to be 10 feet tall.

Once the exterior door of the mudroom opened, it was like nothing I had ever seen. Yes, I had seen this garden many times growing up, but every time I went back to visit her, she always had something new, something blooming or a new story about her plant material.

As a visitor to the enchanted garden, you were first greeted by a kaleidoscope of colors and textures. Next, the gentle aroma of freshness and goodness filled the air no matter the season. She never had plant labels for her plants but she could tell you everything about them from her heart. This included their common and Latin name, growing requirements, planting techniques, seed collection how to, and the most important part-where the plant came from. You see, she could make the deadest stick grow. In doing so, a lot of people gave her plant material that they had given up on. All she needed for her collection were some wet paper towels and a way of getting them back to the enchanted garden.

On the other side of my family tree, I had my grandfather who was a pharmacist by trade but did dabble in gardening. His form of gardening was not haphazard or experimental. It was strictly by the book. No deviation from the cold, hard facts of garden cultivation printed up by many land-grant colleges. These publications were his gardening bible that helped feed, clothe, and house humans. On the other hand, his occupation only helped people with their ailments. These two worlds never came together. As far as he was concerned, they were not even on the same planet, or until his granddaughter asked a question.

Oh and what a question I asked. Being curious and loving many things including nature and history, I asked my grandfather what people did in the past before modern medicine. I remember his reply like it was yesterday. To answer this question, he took my hand and we walked over to the garden swing. As he and I sat down, he began to tell me a story that his grandfather had told him about the relationship between plants and man.

Hundreds of years ago, man appeared on the land. Prior to this, the land was inhabited by animals, plants, and special creatures that took care of all that existed on the earth. These special creatures were gnomes, fairies, and nymphs who had special powers that took care of all living organisms, which included animals, plants, rivers, oceans, stones, soil, and even the stars. As man walked through the land, the plants, animals and the special creatures began to talk. While the humans only heard the wind blow or felt the grass move, the special creatures observed their actions and reported back to all the living creatures they were responsible for. A common theme in this discussion was how weak the humans were. What would happen to them if they got sick? They were not like the trees and other plants that had some natural defense against disease. It seemed to the special creatures that Mother Nature had forgotten about the humans. After a long, global debate, the special creatures decided-with the help of the plants-to teach the humans how to take care of themselves. In doing so, the gnomes, fairies, and nymphs became the guardians of the human species. The plants would make their healing properties known to mankind so that this unique species could thrive in harmony with all other living organisms. This information was carried over to the next generation as oral history and today is called ethnobotany.

Years later, while I was at Purdue I wondered why my interests were so diverse. I mean I was in three different schools at one time! Frankly, no one saw a problem with this. It was just me-a student with diverse interests and passions. This pattern continued when I got my MA. But the story was different. I was told, I really needed to grow up and pick one passion. One interest to follow through the rest of my life seemed to me, to be so boring. How could I do this? How could I just give up on this bonsai creation that my family tree groomed and cared for?

As time went on, I continued walking down my own path; collecting plants, twigs, seedpods just like my great-grandmother. I learned the genealogy of the plants and the science behind their care and growing requirements. As my grandfather reluctantly acknowledged the role of plants in his occupation, I too learned about the old and new uses for all plants. Finally, my diverse education made sense. Now I could provide a historical perspective on plants-based on a series of books that did not add plants into the storyline simply because they rolled off the tongue or looked pretty. The plants themselves became characters with their own individual story to tell. A story that intertwined a scientific question with history, wars, and plants, this story became the conceptual creator of the Outlander Botanist.

INTRODUCTION

In the beginning, the human species shared the earth with beasts and plants. For some reason though, the importance of plants in our survival seemed to be forgotten. Yes, we as a species walked the terra firma in search of food, and along the way nibbled on plants. We, as a species, used plants in every conceivable way. They provided food, and shelter. Plants also allowed us to make clothing along with extras, such as baskets that made our life easier and safer. But along the way as we developed as a species, the plants began to whisper secrets that we had never heard before. We never really knew or understood what they were saying. As we listened, we learned that certain plants would make us well when we were sick. While the plants talked to everyone, only special people could decipher this sacred language. These special individuals were known by several different names depending on the region-which included witchdoctor, shaman, herbalist or healer. Today, this plant and man relationship is called Ethnobotany.

In the past, we as a species depended on natural treatments for ailments, but this all changed after WWI. Unlike other wars, chemical warfare with substances made in laboratories was used to fight. After WWI, chemical development continued and spread into WWII. The skills it took to grow a chemical arsenal were also used in drug development. Now, we had the skills to modernize medicine by mimicking natural products in a laboratory. It was cheaper and viewed as more civilized. We no longer needed wild products to treat illnesses. While the plants still spoke to us, we choose not to listen. It was easier to pop a pill that promised to cure all your aliments.

Presently, this new field has developed some urgency. Urban development and logging is removing plant material at a rate that seems to speed up every year. Those "special" individuals that understood the plants' language are quickly disappearing-and with them so goes the oral history.

The purpose of this book is not to promote herbal cures, even though scientists are finding out that natural treatments are better for the body. The real intention of this book is to provide information on each herb mentioned in the Outlander series of books and the cable show (STARZ) along with how they were used in antiquity and how to grow them. To save you time and energy, sources will be listed for companies that sale seeds of the listed herbs. This list is only created to save you time and I have no affiliation with any of these companies.

GETTING BACK TO THE BASICS

If you have never gotten your hands dirty in the soil, you are really missing out on a wonderful and healthy experience. Yes, I said a healthy experience! Gardening is a wonderful activity that raises your mood while exposing you to an environment that has a unique arrangement of organisms. This diversity of living organisms is what really makes playing in the soil beneficial. It allows us to build a stronger immune system. But, we as a society, have become soilphobic. We are afraid to get dirty or even allow our children to play outside and get grubby.

On the other side of the coin, society has become so removed from the farm that we no longer really know how to grow plants. The idea of growing something from seed or some other type of plant propagation is just as foreign as going to Mars. Programs that used to teach gardening have disappeared as other topics have become more important. The few schools that have cycled back around to the true basic skills have programs run by novice gardeners, and supported through funds that dry up. Once this happens, the gardens will close. And kids, once again, will never be permitted to get dirty.

While gardening programs may come and go, there are individuals out there fighting for the right to grow their own food. Their knowledge base comes from the Internet, books, and fellow gardeners-but not from their elders. This change began in the 70's when mothers really began to work outside the home and everyone became too busy to garden.

Today, there is a swing back to the basics. Boho hair styles, the no washing your hair or body movement-along with organic gardening-are just a few of the actions people are doing that are indicating a change. To insure that this change is correct, we are going to take a look at the basics of gardening. If you are a seasoned gardener, this course will be a refresher course. On the other hand, if you are new to gardening, this primer will give a basic knowledge base by which to grow your own organic garden.

Plant Terminology

Part of learning how to garden starts off with understanding plant terminology. The first terms we will define are those that explain a plant's life cycle. This includes annuals, biennials, and perennials. The bases of these definitions depend on the life cycle of the plant. The life cycle of any plant is the amount of time it takes to grow from a seed to producing seeds. In annuals, this means the life cycle covers one year. Biennials, on the other hand, require two years to mature. Their life cycle starts out with just producing vegetation during their first year of growth. The second year's growth consists of producing more leaves and then a flower stalk. Once the flower stalk has gone to seed, the plant dies. The last life cycle is the perennial. A perennial is any plant that grows for more than two years. It can go to seed but it will return next year from roots.

Another term you will be faced with is organic. If you are buying plants, the term organic means the seed that was used to grow the plant came from parent plants that were not treated with anything made in a chemical lab or inorganic. The plant also needs to be fed only organic fertilizer, and pest issues need to be addressed naturally. Organic seed is seed that comes from plants that were raised without chemical applications of any kind.

Propagating your Plants

Plants can be propagated in several ways; which includes seeds, cuttings, layering, division, bulbs and corms. While we will be talking about growing the herbs from seed, the remaining propagation techniques will be covered for your information.

Propagating plants from seed is the only sexual way that plants propagate.

The remaining forms of plant propagation are through asexual reproduction. What this means is that the propagated part of the plant will be exactly like the plant it came from. The first asexual propagation we will cover is cuttings. This is a general term that refers to removing plant material that will be used to create another plant. This plant material can come from the stem, leaf, and root. The key to this technique is to make sure to dip the cut end into a rooting hormone and then into soil that has been premoistened. Once you have your entire cuttings done, place the container in a clear, plastic bag. This will act as a mini-greenhouse. Move the cutting(s) to a warm location but away from direct sunlight. Depending on the plant material and type of cutting you did, you should expect roots to begin in four to six weeks. To check for this, remove the container from the plastic bag and give a little tug. If you feel resistance then the cutting has began to root.

Layering, on the other hand, requires one to bend the stem of a plant down so that it can touch the soil or simply bury it. This contact will cause the bent material to root. The advantage of layering over cuttings is the fact that the start continues to get water and nutrients from the mother plant.

There are several different types of layerings. This includes simple, tip, compound, and mound. The last type of layering is air. This approach requires one to remove some of the bark from the chosen stem. Once that is done, apply a rooting hormone and cover the cut area with moistened sphagnum moss. Envelop this area with plastic wrap and secure with garden ties. Depending on the plant, you should see roots forming in 1 to 3 months.

If you are looking for a way of creating a new plant instantly, then division propagation is for you. What is division propagation? Well, it is the process by which you dig up the mother plant, split the root mass in half and replant the two parts separately.

The last propagation technique is through bulbs and corms. While these two terms are sometimes used in interchangeable ways, the real difference can be seen when you cut them in half. Bulbs are essentially layers of modified leaves while corms are actually a plant stem. As the corm grows, roots come out the bottom and leaves will appear from buds that are located on the top of the corm.

When it comes to growing plants from bulbs or corms the process is easy and only requires one to plant the structure in the soil at the prescribed depth. As the bulb or corm grows, it will produce bulblets or cormels, which are offshoots. These offshoots can then be removed and replanted.

Seed Propagation Primer

When it comes to starting plants from seed, there are a few supplies you will need beyond the seed. First, it you are not directly seeding into the ground, you will need a container. You can create one with newspapers or upcycled containers in your kitchen. This includes paper cups, and food storage containers. Other choices for containers include seed sowing flats, peat pots, peat pellets, and peat plugs. Each one of these container types have their own pros and cons but there are two keys by which you need to follow that will make selection easier. First, the container of choice needs to have good drainage. All the above containers have good drainage except the food storage containers. To meet this requirement, holes will have to be made in the container. Second, if you are starting seeds that do not like to be transplanted, then you will need to use the peat pots, pellets or plugs.

If using anything in plastic or terra cotta, you will need to sterilize it. The process is simple. Fill a basin of water and add a capful or two of bleach. Place the container in the water and allow it to soak for a few minutes. Next, take a scrub brush and remove any dirt off the container. Once the container is clean, you will need to rinse it in clear water and place it in the sun if possible. While this may seem a little odd, the exposure to sunlight will aid in the sterilization process.

Now that you have your container, let's talk about what goes inside it. There are several different planting mediums and ingredients to choose from. This includes peat moss, sphagnum moss, vermiculite, and perlite.

Bagged or baled peat moss is decomposed aquatic plants that are used in planting medium mixtures. It does hold water but the level is not reliable. On the other hand, sphagnum moss can hold 10 to 20 times its weight in water. In doing so, it can be used as a seed starting planting medium but has no plant nutrients.

Vermiculite is expanded mica that can hold unbelievable amounts of water. It also contains plant nutrients magnesium and potassium, which are important for root development. But this ingredient is normally not used by itself.

Perlite is volcanic ash. The importance of this ingredient is the fact that it remains cool. This can be an important factor when you are starting seeds that require cooler temperatures. But perlite does have a negative aspect. When water is added to this ingredient it floats.

Since each ingredient has its own pros and cons, a mixture is the best approach. If you are looking for a DIY seed starting medium, begin with ½ peat or sphagnum moss to equal amounts of vermiculite or perlite. You can also use a combination of vermiculite and perlite. If you do not want to make your own seed starting medium, there are several commercial types available.

Once you are ready to start your seeds, moisten the seed starting medium with water. The reason for this is the fact that some seeds are very small and if watered from the top would be carried down through the soil. Using soil that is already moist is a way of avoiding this problem.

Next, add your moistened soil to your container, and gently tap on a hard surface to settle the soil. Now you are ready to plant.

There is a set depth by which each seed needs to be planted. This information can be found on the seed package but a golden rule to follow is the seed needs to be at a depth that is equal to four times its diameter.

After the seed has been planted, gently push down on the soil surface to make sure that the seed has contact with the soil. If the seed is small, simply mist the soil surface with water. For larger seeds, water the soil from the top until you see moisture come out the bottom of the container.

At this point, do not forget to make a plant label. While you may say you will remember what you planted, chances are this is not true. If you do not want to go out and buy labels, make them from old corks, broken pots, and even tape. Regardless of the material you use, make sure to include the name of the plant along with the planting date.

If you are a forgetful gardener, you can place your planted container in a clear plastic bag. Tie the bag off and place in an area by which the bag will not be exposed to direct sunlight. Once you see your plants germinating, remove the bag and move to a location where the seedlings can receive the required sunlight.

Beyond sunlight, seeds need a temperature around 70 to 75 degrees Fahrenheit to germinate. After they have germinated, most seedlings like a temperature of between 60 and 70 degrees Fahrenheit.

The other requirement is moisture. While the planted seeds were in the plastic bag, moisture level and humidity was fine but once the container is taken out of the bag, you need to watch the soil moisture daily. You can test the soil moisture with your finger by sticking it straight into the soil and then pulling straight up. If your finger comes out clean then you need to water. Another way is to look at the soil. A dry soil will be lighter color compared to a damp one.

While this is the basic instructions for planting seeds, some seeds need a little help from Mother Nature. To mimic these environmental conditions, several techniques are used. One of the easiest is to simply soak the seed in water overnight. The next day the seed will be ready to plant. Stratification is the process by which you expose seed to heat or cold. This mimics the natural seasonal change of the environment. The temperature required is dependent on the seed. To begin the process, one will need to add moistened peat moss or vermiculite to a container or sealable plastic bag. Next, add the seed and seal. If you need heat, simply place the prepared container in a warm room. On the other hand, if you need to mimic cold, just put the planted container in the refrigerator or freezer if colder temperatures are required. Keep in the required location for the set time period, which can be a few weeks to a few months. Periodically, pull your container out and look for small, white primary roots. If you see these, plant the seeds as soon as possible.

The last treatment is scarification, which mimics the chewing of animals on the seed coat. The easiest way to do this is to just nick the seed coat with a file or knife. This will make it easier for the plant to get through the seed coat.

Once you have your seeds planted and they have germinated, what is next? The first thing you will need to do is to start feeding after the first true leaves appear. No, the first leaves are not the true leaves but leaves that temperately feed the seedling. Prior to that feeding source drying up, the plant begins to form true leaves.

To help feed the fast growing plant, begin to feed your seedlings with ¼ the strength of a water soluble balanced fertilizer. What is a balanced fertilizer? It is one that all the numbers are the same. As the seedlings get more leaves, increase the dilution to ½ the full strength. If you are using peat pots, pellets and/or plugs, add the diluted fertilizer to a separate container and place the planted pot in the container for bottom watering.

If you have planted your seeds in individual peat pots, pellets and/or plugs, you will not need to transplant them. On the other hand, if you planted your seeds in flats or containers, you will need to move the seedlings into individual containers as soon as they have four true leaves.

When performing this task, do not pull the seedlings out by their stem or leaves. The best approach to remove them from their container is to first water the soil. Once the soil is completely moist, slide the handle of a fork or spoon under the plants roots and lift up. If you have a group of seedlings come up, gently separate them making sure not to tear the roots. After that is done, plant the seedlings in individual containers. Please keep in mind though that the best way of handling your seedlings is not by the stems instead gently hold them by their leaves.

Regardless of how you have propagated your plant material, if it was kept indoors it will need to be hardened off. This is a process by which you slowly expose the plant material to the outdoor environment. This should be done over a one to two week period. The purpose of this process is to toughen up the tissue of the stem so that it can handle the harsher outdoor environment.

To start the hardening off process, first place the plants outside for a few hours on a cloudy day. As the days progress, move the plant material closer to their planned new home. Continue to do this until your seedlings stay out for 24 hours but if a frost is in the forecast, do not forget to bring them in.

Once the seedlings have been hardened off and your local frost-free date has passed, they are prepared to grow outside in your garden or container.

When it comes to planting your seeds directly into a garden space, the steps are different. Since this book is designed for urban and landless gardeners, a brief summary will be given on traditional gardening.

The first step to planting directly into the ground is the garden preparation. This begins by removing all the unwanted plant material, and digging down at least eight inches but preferably12. The reason the depth is so deep is so that the soil is loose for the roots of the plant to penetrate. This process can be done by hand or tiller. While digging up the garden, you can add well seasoned compost and/or manure to the soil. This will enrich the soil along with adding beneficial bacteria and/or fungus to the earth. Keep in mind though; this must be done with seasoned organic matter. While compost that is not seasoned will through your soil nutrient level off, it will not burn the plant material like "hot" or non-seasoned manure. What does seasoned mean? Well, it describes organic material that has sat for at least one year.

Once that is done, smooth the surface over. Now plan your garden space on paper, making sure to allow the proper spacing for each seed/plant you plan on planting. To make caring for your traditional garden easier, plant your seeds/plants in rows that are marked with a plant label. Creating these rows is simple and only requires stakes and string. Measure off the length of the row you want. Place a stake at each end, and tie a string to each stake.

Next, mark where each individual seed/plant will go with a circle of powdered milk. Once this is done, you can begin to plant your traditional garden.

When planting in a traditional garden, keep in mind that once your seeds have been planted, make sure to go over the area with a shovel or hoe pressing down on the soil. This will make sure that your seed makes contact with the soil. Also, only water after all your seeds have been planted.

At this point, you may be wondering about the watering of a traditional garden. It is very important to keep the soil evenly moist and in early spring, this is normally not a problem since spring rains keep the soil most. On the other hand, planting later on in the season can create an issue when it comes to watering. The best suggestion I have when it comes to watering is two-fold.

First, place a rain gauge near your garden. A good rule of thumb is one to two inches of rain a week. The second prong of this approach is the old-finger test. Utilizing both of these will help you decide if you need to water or not. As your plants mature, it will be easier to tell if they need to be watered due to appearance of drooping leaves and stems.

Once you have planted and watered your traditional garden, you can remove the stakes if you like, but make sure to keep the plant labels in the ground.

Creating a garden space from scratch is a lot of work but there are a few tips and strategies that make it easier.

The first technique by which one can create a traditional garden space is through soil sterilization. This process entails one covering the planned garden space with sheets of cardboard and topping this layer with black plastic. Allow this to sit for several weeks. What happens is that the black plastic heats up. This heat kills anything under the plastic. This includes plants, seeds, animals, bacteria, and fungi. While you can simply put the plastic down on the ground, you are running into an issue of contaminating your soil with toxins from the hot plastic. Placing the cardboard first absorbs these toxins. While this works, you still need to go in and loosen the soil. You will also need to add seasoned compost and/or manure to add back into the soil for the beneficial flora and fauna.

You can artificially create your garden through lasagna gardening. This must be planned out a year in advance, and preferably in the fall. While there are several different recipes for lasagna gardening, the easiest one I have found for urban gardeners is this one, which really does not take excessive amounts of extra supplies.

The first thing you need to do is to mark off the garden space with rope or simply a powdered milk line. Next, lay down five to seven layers of newspaper, or one layer of corrugated cardboard.

Completely saturate the paper or cardboard with water. The next layer is what is called the "green" layer. This is organic material that you would put in your compost bin. Ideas for this layer include kitchen scraps, grass clippings, fresh manure from herbivores, and even coffee/tea grounds. Once you have completely covered the newspaper/cardboard layer with the "green" compost, add "brown" compost. This includes dried leaves, hay and/or shredded newspaper. Continue to add these ingredients until the "green" compost is covered. Repeat the process until the pile is 18 to 24 inches in height. After that height has been reached, stop adding material and allow the lasagna garden to season. Next spring it will be ready to plant.

Planting into a lasagna garden is easy. There are two approaches. One is to dig down to the first layer, and plant. The material that you move is simply mulch that you place around the plants. The second approach is to just break up the layers. Once that's done, just plant directly into the layers. Either approach works but for weed control, I have found that planting directly into the layers works best.

A raised bed is another choice. While your bed can be any length, to be able to reach the center it should only be four feet wide. Also, used non-pressure treated wood if you plan on eating anything out of the garden. Finally, to aid in weed control, do two things.

First, when you place your raised beds in your garden space make sure to lay down landscape cloth first. This will prevent weeds from growing from the ground up into the bed.

The second thing you can do is to simply seal it up when your growing season is done. To do this, place corrugated cardboard on top of the soil in the raised bed. Top this with black plastic, and secure it to the raised bed with stones or staple into the sides of the bed. This simple step will sterilize the soil for next season while preventing weed seeds from blowing in onto the soil.

Straw bale gardening is another approach to creating a garden space. There are two key points when it comes to utilizing this technique. First, make sure you get straw and not hay. Straw is the stalks leftover in the field after the grain has been harvested. It contains very few weed seeds. On the other hand, hay is grass that is mowed down and bundled up after it has dried. The problem with using hay as your garden base is the fact that it is full of weed seeds.

The second key point is to plan ahead if you are going to use this technique. The straw bale will need to season for three weeks prior to planting. When using this approach, first place your straw bale in the location where the environmental conditions are right for what you want to plant. Next, Place your straw bale so that the narrow end is up and the stalks are cut side up. Having the cut side of the bale up will allow the hollow tubes of the grain stalks to collect water.

Once you have done this step, you are ready to condition the bale. Since straw is a natural material, it will begin to break down. This decomposition process is hot and can easily kill your plants if you plant into the bale at this time. The best approach is to condition the bale or speed up the decomposition process.

To begin, for the next four days, only water the straw bales. Then, for the next six to seven days, sprinkle with a water soluble, balanced fertilizer, such as a 10-10-10. If you do not want to go this route, you can dissolve the fertilizer in water and apply it to the bales.

Repeat this process until three weeks have passed. At this point, the bale should not feel hot nor should you see steams coming up from the bale. At this point you are ready to plant.

Planting in a seasoned straw bale is simple. If you are planting seed, just make a hole in the bale, add a little soil and plant your seed. Plants are planted in the bale the same way except soil is not added.

Caring for this type of garden is easy. Only water the straw bale garden when the straw feels dry. This will not occur very often since straw stays moist longer.

When it comes to fertilizing, you will not need to do it as often or not at all since the straw itself provides fertilizer.

Once the season is over, dismantle your straw bales. Add the contents to your compost bin or use the spent straw as mulch around other plants.

When, Where, and How to Plant

As the saying goes, there is a season for everything and gardening is no exception. But how do you know when to start seeds and/or plants? The answer is simple and it has to do with the area by which you live. Every area has a frost-free date. This date is the last time you can expect to have a frost. While there are unusual times when a freak frost occurs, in general you can go by this date.

To find out your local frost-free date, click on this link. Once you are there, type in the search box your state. Then, click on frost/free occurrence data and find the city closest to your location. The category of 10 percent is your local frost-free date.

Now that you have your local frost-free date, you can plan on when to plant outside. This information can also be used to plan when to plant indoors.

In general, you will need to count back from your local frost-free date six to eight weeks. The date you come up with is your seed starting date. Do not get hung up on this date. You can fluctuate a week or two and still be successful.

Where to plant is based on your area along with the sun requirement. The where that I am talking about has to do with your plant hardiness zone. All plants have a range by which they can grow. What creates this range is your area's coldest temperature average. Some plants are limited to one zone while others will be listed by a range of zones. Just keep in mind that the larger the number of hardiness zone the milder the coldest temperature will be.

Click on the Interactive USDA Plant Hardiness Zone Map and type in your zip code. This simple step will provide you with the plant hardiness zone of your area.

Another question you will be faced with is when it comes to the sunlight requirement. There are three choices when one is talking about sun exposure. The first one is full sun, which can be defined as at least six hours of direct sun every day. Partial shade/partial sun can be defined by three to six hours of direct sunlight. Shade means that the area receives less than three hours of sunlight a day. But keep in mind that as the season goes from spring to summer and then fall to winter, the amount of sunlight exposure can change. The best way is to observe your garden, make notes of where the sun hits your garden space and for how long over the course of a year. While things like new buildings and plant material can change this information, it is an excellent tool by which you can plan your garden space by sunlight requirement.

The last question that remains is how to place a plant in the ground properly. This is one of the steps that a lot of people skimp on. They think that you just dig a hole, and place your plant inside. While this is the basic principle, there are a few steps that will make your plant happier-which in turn will make you a better gardener.

The first step is the hole size. It needs to be the same depth as the container that the plant is presently in. The width of the hole needs to be two to three times the width of the container. While the width may seem excessive, the reason for this measurement is so that the roots can grow outward into loosened soil. If you have a lot of clay in your soil, you will need to do an extra step. This step is referred to as deglazing the hole, which requires one to take a rake, and scrape the inside of the hole. This scraping roughs up the clay inside the hole enough so that it does not become smooth like a terra cotta pot.

Once you have the hole dug, place the container with the plant in it in the hole to test the size. Adjust the hole as needed. The next step is to remove the plant from the container but there is one exception. If you are using peat pots, do not take the plants out of the container. How to plant a peat pot will be covered later.

Removing a plant from its container can be a tricky task. You do not want to damage the leaves, stem and/or roots during this process. The easiest way of doing this is to simply cut slits down the sides of the container and peel the container away from the roots. This technique only works with plastic pots. If you want to save the container or you are using a terra cotta container, the other technique requires one to tip the container upside down while holding the plant. Next, gently tap the bottom of the container. If it the container is plastic, you can even squeeze the sides. If the plant will not come out, take a table knife and run it on the inside of the pot. Repeat the process until the plant has come out into your hand.

Once the plant has been removed from the pot, you will need to tease the roots. This process simply means that you loosen the root mass with your fingers. If this is not done, you are running the risk of the roots continuing to grow in the shape of the pot and not grow outwards. While there is no steadfast rule on how much teasing needs to be done, keep in mind that you need to be gentle so that you do not destroy the root ball.

After the roots have been teased place the plant in the prepared hole. Fill in with soil and gently push down on the hole with a hand spade or shovel. Water the soil at this point. You may find that the soil level drops after watering. Do not worry. The water pushes out air bubbles, which will lower the soil level. Add soil as needed to get the soil level up to the plant's planted level in the container.

When it comes to peat pots, you do not remove the plant from the container. The reason for this is the fact that the peat pot is a natural product that will breakdown. To help your plant's roots break through the sides of the peat pot, make a few slits in the sides with a pair of scissors. While you can use a knife, you do run the chance of going too deep into the root ball. Once that is done, you are ready to plant your peat pot.

There is one more step in this process. Peat has a tendency to wick moisture. In doing so, make sure that the top of the peat pot is under the soil. If you find that your plant is planted too deep using this approach, simply cut or tear the top until you reach a level by which the peat pot is under the soil. Water and adjust the soil level as described previously.

AGRIMONY

Agrimonia eupatoria

Agrimony is an herb that has a long history with the Greeks, Romans, Europeans, and even in America. The term agrimony comes from the Greek word argemone, which means "plants that are healing to the eye." The latter term, eupatoria, comes from the King Mithridates Eupator of Pontus, which was located in ancient Persia. He was said to have come up with a universal antidote to poison using the agrimony.

When it comes to alternative names for this herb, you can find it under the names Church Steeples, Liverwart, Cocklebur, and Sticklewart. The latter names explain the plants ability to spread. The seed capsules have burrs on them that allow the seed to attach to clothing and fur. This is one of the reasons why this plant easily disperses through the environment.

As the Latin name implies, this herb has been used to treat eye problems along with diarrhea, athlete's foot, asthma, coughs, fevers, and skin diseases. This may be why Claire included it in her medical kit in Paris (Dragonfly in Amber, chapter 22).

Alternative uses for this herb can be found in witchcraft where it was believed to create a protect shield for spells. It was used to clean the aura of the body and tools along with adding strength to spells that were cast for healing purposes.

This perennial can easily be grown in USDA Plant Hardiness Zones 5 through 9. As far as propagation techniques go, agrimony can be started by seed or division. When it comes to planting the seed, the first step of this process is to expose them to the cold or through cold stratification. To begin this process, you will first need to fill a small, plastic bag that is resealable with either premoistened potting soil or vermiculite. Once that is done, bury your seeds in this moistened planting medium and place in the refrigerator for four to eight weeks prior to your local frost-free date. Check the bag frequently to make sure the planting medium has not dried out. Add water as needed.

While you are cold stratifying your seeds, pick out the best gardening spot for your agrimony. This herb requires full sun but can tolerate a little shade. As far as the soil goes, it really needs a well-draining soil that is calcareous with a little sand mixed in. Once this location has been picked, prepare it as needed for your agrimony seedlings.

While you have checked your seeds in the refrigerator, you may find that some have germinated. If this is the case, plant these immediately. To plant your agrimony seeds, start off with filling your container with an all-purpose potting soil. Next, sprinkle the seeds on top of this medium and cover with ¼ inch of soil. Place your seeded containers in a sunny location. Keep the soil moist but not wet. In 10 to 25 days, you should see little green dots appear on the soil surface. These dots are your germinated seeds. Once that happens, continue to care for your seeds and after the weather warms in the spring, harden the seedlings off.

Plant the seedlings in the garden space after they have been harden off and have reached the height of four-inches.

When it comes to planting this herb in your garden space, make sure to give them some room. Agrimony requires 12 to 36 inches between plants. This gives this plant plenty of room to grow out since it can reach heights of 20 feet or more at maturity.

If you desire to divide agrimony, the process is simple. Dig up the plant and remove the suckers off the Mother plant. When using this approach, make sure that the suckers have roots attached. Once this is done, replant your divided agrimony.

ALOE

Aloe barbadenis

Aloe is a familiar houseplant that has many names, which include Aloe Vera, Lily of the Desert, Burn Plant, and Aloe Africana just to name a few. This plant is considered a perennial and can successful be grown outside in USDA Plant Hardiness Zones 10 through 12.

This succulent herb is considered a subtropical and tropical plant that can be found growing wild in Latin America, Southern Africa, and the Caribbean.

As far as the uses of this herb in history, this plant was very commonly prescribed during the 18th and 19th century for many illnesses. While you may be familiar with aloe being used for burns and skin irritations, aloe can also be used to treat herpes.

The soothing nature of this herb is why Claire used it on Jamie's back while they were at the Abby of the Ste. Anne de Beaupre (Outlander, chapter 40).

The juice from the aloe reappears as a soothing treatment for the rash associated with nettle exposure. Claire used the gel of this plant to treat Jamie's nettle rash along with hers, which she received when Jamie threatened to beat her with the nettles (Dragonfly in Amber, chapter 29). Claire also shares the knowledge that aloe gel treats burns (Voyager, chapter 27).

Claire applies an aloe ointment to a child who receiving treatment for burns at the L'Hopital des Anges (Dragonfly in Amber, chapter 12).

When it comes to growing and caring for aloe, the process is simple. Unless you live in USDA Plant Hardiness Zones 10 and 11, you will need to grow your plant inside. It requires a warm environment and a location that receives indirect sunlight.

Aloe is only propagated through the removal of offsets, pups, or plantlets, which are small individual plants that come off the mother plant. When removing the plantlets, do not just pull them off. Take a knife and cut the plantlet away from the mother plant. When doing this, make sure that you also have root attached. Let the removed plantlets set out for a day to callus over.

Once that is done, it is time to prepare the container. You will need to make sure that it is wide container. The reason for this is the fact that aloe tends to grow outward or spread. The other container characteristic that you need to have is a drainage hole. Since aloe is considered a succulent, it does not like to have its soil wet. Having a drainage hole in the bottom of the container will allow the excess water to flow out.

Now that you have your container, add drainage material and fill with cactus or succulent potting medium. Add your callused aloe plantlets to the container making sure the roots are covered.

Additional care that aloes require is watering. Unlike other houseplants, aloe may not need to be watered weekly. The first watering should be thoroughly so that water comes out the drainage hole. Do not water again until the soil is dry at least one to two inches deep. Water again once this condition has been met.

While you may be tempted to fertilize your aloe, it is not necessary.

ANGELICA

Angelica archangelica

As unique as the name is, so is whether it is a biennial or perennial. The growth habit of this plant starts off with vegetative growth the first year. The second year it will reappear and flower. Once the seeds have ripened, the plant will die. By definition, this is a biennial but there is still controversy out there.

The history of this plant is very interesting and starts off with a monk taking a nap. During his nap, an angel entered his dreams with a message. The angel identified a plant that was the cure for the plague. From then on, the plant was known as angelica. It was also named the most powerful herb and in doing so received the nickname "Root of the Holy Ghost."

This plant was also believed to be under the protection of Michael the Archangel since it bloomed on May 8th according to the old Julian calendar, which is also Michael's feast day.

While the ancients believed this herb could cure anything and used it as a defense against evil spirits, spells, and even witches, it is mostly used to treat excessive flatulence, female reproductive issues, indigestion, chronic bronchitis, and joint pain. Today, herbalists make an oil using angelica to treat joint pain.

The multi-symptom uses of this herb may be why it was part of Davie Beaton's surgery (Outlander, chapter 7).

Since this plant has moved through the cool European climates, this also explains why it was found growing alongside the path to the Saint's pool where Dougal took Claire after she saw Jack Randall (Outlander, chapter 13).

Angelica appears as part of the ingredients for a tea that would treat constipation. Beyond this herb, Claire combines anise peppermint, and horehound creating a tea that she gives Duncan Innes for constipation (Voyager, chapter 43).

While this plant can be divided, the best way to propagate this herb is through seed. Many sources talk about the difficulty in getting angelica seed to germinate but there is a trick. The seed must be fresh. In doing so, be careful when you purchase seed.

The best approach is to harvest your own and replant that season. If that is not possible, simply freeze the seeds until spring and then plant.

Planting angelica seed should be done outside. While some individuals have had some success in starting angelica indoors, the problem lies when you go to plant them outside. Most angelica seedlings and plants do not do well with transplanting. To have the most success in growing this plant, sow your seeds outside as soon as they are ripe off the plant. This should be in August to September. The area needs to receive bright sunlight but can have a few dabbles of shade. The soil needs to be moist and loamy but not standing in water. The hardiness for this plant can be found in the USDA Plant Hardiness Zones 5 through 9.

Since this seed is known to have a low germination rate, simply broadcast over the prepared garden bed. Once that is done, top the seed with a fine layer of soil that is less than ¼ inch. After the seeds have germinated, thin out the seedlings so that there is 18 inches between the plants. Later on in the season, thin the plants again so that there is a total of three feet between each herb. The reason for this space is the fact that the branches of this herb can span three feet and the plant can reach heights up to six feet.

While you may feel that due to this plant's size, the only way to use it in the garden is as a specimen plant. Yes, it could be used for that but there are other plants that can be planted with it to make it a part of your landscape. This includes ferns, hellebores, and sweet woodruff.

As far as any extra care this herb requires, there are two things. One, angelica does not tolerate dry conditions. In doing so, monitor the moisture level of the soil and water as needed. The second task that will need to be done is to cut the flower stalk as soon as the seeds have ripened. The reason for this is three-fold.

First, the plant's life cycle is ending and two, unless you want angelica everywhere you will need to harvest the seed head. The third reason has to do with extending the life of the plant. Some believe that removing the flower head before the flowers open will extend the life of the plant. There is not adequate evidence to prove this since this plant is considered a short lived perennial or biennial.

ANISE

Pimpinella anisum

This herb may be one that you have heard of that tastes like black licorice. It can be found in the culinary world as a flavoring for liquors, alcohols, meats, dairy products, and even in breath fresheners. Since anise is an aromatic herb, it can also be found in soaps, sachets, and perfumes.

Anise has graced English gardens since the sixteenth century. In the past, anise was not only used in the kitchen but also as a poison for mice and pigeons. It was believed to kill mice put anise oil on the trap smeared as bait. Anise has also been found to work as an insecticide.

This herb has also been used in the nontraditional realm as a way of averting the Evil Eye.

While consuming anise was known to treat a sour stomach, it can also be used as a diuretic, appetite stimulant, to increase the flow of milk while breastfeeding, start menstruation, aid in childbirth, and even as a treatment for male menopause. Another unlikely use for anise comes when it is applied to the skin. In this approach, it can be a treatment for lice, psoriases, and scabies.

The many medical uses this herb has is why Claire found it in buckets of water in Haugh's Apothecary (Voyager, chapter 24). She also notes the aroma of this herb emitting from Haugh's apothecary shop when she travels beck through the stones (Voyager, chapter 29). When Duncan Innes became constipated,

Claire treated him with a tea made from angelica, horehound, peppermint, and anise or aniseed, which is another name for this herb (Voyager, chapter 43). The culinary value of this herb is why Claire was able to bribe the cook Mr. Murphy with anise while on board the Artenis (Voyager, Chapter 41).

When it comes to growing this herb in your home garden, you will need to start the process off six to eight weeks prior to your local frost-free date. This allows you to get a jump on the 60 day maturity time of this herb. Since this annual herb is known to suffer from transplanting shock, the planting technique will be a little different. What you will need to do first is to fill biodegradable pots with a good, all-purpose potting soil. Once that is done, sprinkle your seeds on the soil surface and cover with ¼ inch of soil.

After all your biodegradable pots have been planted, place them in a tray and add water. This is a simple technique by which you can water your anise without drowning the seeds. Next, move them to a warm location that is kept around 70 degrees Fahrenheit. In 10 to 14 days, you should see little green dots appear on the soil surface.

Continue to monitor soil moisture. Once the anise seedlings are four to five-inches in height and have their first set of true leaves, it is time to harden them off.

After the seedlings have been hardened off, it is time to plant them in the garden, but pick you day and location wisely. To reduce transplanting stress, choose to plant your seedlings when it is overcast or cloudy. As far as the location goes, anise likes a sunny location with a well-draining soil. It also prefers a soil with a lot of organic matter. To meet this requirement, simply mix in a good amount of well seasoned compost before planting in your garden space.

When planting this herb in the garden, make sure to leave 12 inches between plants and 18 to 24 inches between rows. This will give the anise plenty of room to grow 18 inches or more outward without causing problems.

If you do not have garden space for this plant, do not hesitate to plant it in a container that is at least eight inches deep and wide.

Once your anise is planted, you will need to monitor soil moisture and water when the soil is dry. Anise does not need to be fertilized every month but a simple side dressing of well seasoned compost will aid in its production if applied in the middle of the growing season. One special treatment that anise does require is staking of the flower heads. This is especially true if you live in a windy location.

If you are looking for companion plantings for your anise, consider combining it with cabbage, grapes or coriander. This latter has been found to improve the formation of the anise seed. To maximize the growth of your anise, rotate every other year with herbs such as basil.

BASIL

Ocimum basilicum

As you may know, basil is a well known herb used in cooking. The aromatic properties of this herb are why it was so easy to identify in Geille's stillroom (Outlander, chapter 9). This same aromatic property is why basil is so healthy for you. When eaten, it can protect your DNA along with fighting off several species of bacteria that have become antibiotic resistant. Basil has also been found to reduce inflammation and be good for the heart. The latter use comes from basil's beta-carotene and its ability to calm one down when consumed.

The herb is one of the easiest to grow. It can be propagated from seed and even cuttings. When it comes to propagating your basil from seed, you need to first decide if you want to get a jump on the season or plant directly into the garden space. Since this seed germinates so quickly, I would suggest that you directly seed into the garden space but other approaches will be covered.

When it comes to starting your basil indoors, the first step of this process is to pull out the calendar and decide on a planting date. If the goal is to plant the basil in the garden, you will need to plant your basil inside six to eight weeks prior to your local frost-free date. You may also want to add a week or two to that date since the soil will need to be 70 degrees Fahrenheit before you can safely plant your seedlings in the ground.

Once your selected date has arrived, the next step is to prepare your container and plant your seed. Any container will do as long as it is clean. Next, fill the container with an all-purpose potting soil medium and tap down. Now to get the most out of your seed, pull out your ruler and lay it down on the soil's surface. The reason you are doing this is so that you can properly space out the seed, which means each seed needs to be 6 to 10 inches apart. After all the seeds have been planted, top the seeds with less than ¼ inch of soil and water. Place the planted container on a sunny windowsill. In five days, you should see your little basil seedlings begin to appear.

Continue to monitor the soil moisture and move the seedlings to the garden space after they have been hardened off and you are free of any chance of a frost.

When directly seeding your basil into your garden space, you will first need to select the best location. This means a well-draining soil that is exposed to the sun for at least six to eight hours a day. Once the garden site has been selected, prepare the garden space as usual. Plant your seeds so that they are 6 to 10 inches apart. Water in the seeds and monitor the soil's moisture throughout the growing season. Never let the soil dry out.

If you do not have room in your garden for basil or you just want some for your indoor gardening pleasure, consider growing this annual herb in a container. Since this herb likes to grow tall and wide, you will need at least a 12 inch container. This container size will only hold one plant.

Once you have selected your container, clean it, add drainage material and fill with a good, all-purpose potting soil. Plant seeds as described above or take cuttings. To do this, take your basil and select the best branches from the plant. After you have made the selection, take a three to four-inch cutting from each branch. When taking cutting always make sure that it is done at an angle. Remove all the leaves from the cutting except the top three to four leaves. Also, pinch off any flower stalk that may have grown. After the leaves have been removed, dip the cut end in a rooting hormone. To make a hole for the basil in the soil, take a pencil and make a hole. Next, place the cut end in the hole and gently move the soil around it. Continue with this process until all the cuttings have been used.

At this point, place your container in a tray and fill the tray with water. This will allow you to water from the bottom up without washing off the rooting hormone. Place the planted container in a sunny location and monitor the soil moisture. Water the basil cuttings as needed.

Do not have seeds or cuttings; consider visiting your local produce department for some fresh herbs. Basil snippets from this department can be used as cuttings.

When it comes to caring for your basil, the steps are easy. First, never allow the soil to dry out but do not let it get soggy.

Second, remove any flower stalk when it appears. Third, feed your basil a balanced fertilizer.

If you want to get the most out of your space, plant basil alongside your tomatoes. The basil will improve the taste of the tomatoes while providing protection from certain tomato pests.

BAY LEAF

Laurus nobilisis

The Latin name of bay leaf is very interesting. *Laurus* means to laud or praise while *nobilisis* can be translated to mean noble. The story as to how this herb made its way to Greece starts off with a beautiful nymph called Daphne. As Ovid tells it, the bay leaf was made from Daphne's body. Both Greek and Roman cultures use a crowning wreath of bay leaves as a symbol for victory. Today, boughs of the bay leaf make up part of Greece's national emblem.

Even today, if you are looking for bay leaf in Greece you will find that it goes by the name Daphne. Other names this plant goes by includes sweet bay, Grecian laurel, and bay laurel.

In the past, this herb was used to treat ailments of the kidney, stomach, and liver. Today, some use this herb to reduce fevers, treat colds, and to reduce pain from headaches and arthritic issues.

If you are lucky enough to live in USDA Plant Hardiness Zones 8 through 11then you can leave your bay leaf outside. On the other hand, if you live in any other area then you will need to bring your herb in when the temperature drops.

The only form of propagation for this plant is through cuttings or air layering. For discussion, we will only cover cuttings but visit the section on "Getting Started" for details on how to air layer.

To begin the planting process, starts off with preparing the container. This container can be a flat or pot. It does not matter which you pick but it will need to be cleaned and sterilized. While the container is drying, take a large bucket and combine equal parts of all-purpose potting soil and vermiculite. Mix well and then add water to the planting medium. Repeat this latter process until the entire planting medium is evenly moist. Once that is done, fill the container with this made planting medium.

Next, take several six-inch cuttings from a bay laurel shrub. Make sure when doing this process that the cut is at an angle. Once you have all your cuttings, remove all the leaves except the top two leaves. Cut these remaining leaves horizontally.

After this has been done, you are ready to dip the cuttings in liquid rooting hormone but before you do this make sure to read the directions.

At this stage, you are ready to plant your semi-hardwood cuttings in the container but do not just stick them in. To keep the rooting compound on the stem, take a pencil and poke a hole in the soil to a depth of three inches. The next step is to simply put in the hole. Repeat this process but space out the cuttings so that they do not touch.

Once all the cuttings are in the container, water until you see moisture coming out the bottom of the pot. The next step is to place the container in a plastic bag and seal it up. This will act as a greenhouse. Place the planted greenhouse on a propagation mat that is set at 70 degrees Fahrenheit. If you do not have one, simply place the container in a warm room in a location that receives indirect sunlight.

Check the cuttings often and remove any that seem to be dying. Water the container as need. In about a month, check your cuttings to test the rooting progress. How do you do this? Well, you simply give each cutting a tug. If a cutting gives a little resistance then it is developing roots.

Transplant your cuttings into their own containers when the roots are one inch in length.

Unless you live in an area by which bay leaf can remain outside, you will only want to move your plant outdoors after your local frost-free date has passed and the plant has been hardened off. When it comes to moving it outside, pick a very sunny location that has a very well-draining soil. This soil needs to be so well-draining that the bay leaf is often used in xeriscape design. When you first set out your bay leaf in your garden, water often so that the plant sets out a strong root system. After that, water as needed to keep the soil moist but not wet.

As far as any additional care goes, you will want to fertilize your bay leaf with a balanced fertilizer once a month during the spring and summer months. To keep it from reaching its 60 foot mature size, you will want to prune it.

If your bay leaf is going to solely live in a container, make sure to use the proper soil mix. To keep the soil moist but well-draining, you will need to combine equal parts of cactus mix and an all-purpose potting soil or one part sand to two parts all-purpose potting soil.

Believe it or not, bay leaf is used in the culinary field not for taste but for smell. This is very important since we decide on what we are going to eat by what we see and smell. This is the reason why the smell of bay leaf was recognized in Geillie's clothes (Outlander, chapter 24)..

BETONY

Stachys officinalis

When it comes to betony, you may find that it has different names. First, there are five species of *Stachys* that grow wild in England. While this particular Wood Betony will grow in North America up to USDA Plant Hardiness Zone 4, its wild equivalent is *Pedicularis canaddensis.*

Initially, this plant was referred to as *Betonica officinalis* by Linnaeus. This was then changed to *Stachys betonica.* Today, wood betony can be found as *Stachys officinalis.*

As far as past uses for betony, this herb was so valuable that Italian's developed a proverb. "Sell your coat to buy betony." The importance of this herb can be seen when one visits past monastery and apothecary gardens. Wood betony can still be found growing wild in many of these places due to human intervention.

The vast uses for this herb ranged from chasing evil spirits away to stomach problems and headaches. The latter use for this herb, some believe, comes from the Celtic word bewton, which can be translated as "good for the head."

In the series, betony is mentioned several times. It was found growing in the herb garden at Castle Leoch (Outlander only, chapter 9). Geillis (Outlander, chapter 9) believed that wood betony would turn pigeons into toads, which is a hint to what was believed to be the supernatural powers of this herb. The last mention of this herb goes back to a true use. When betony is taken excessively, it can be used as a way of purging one's system or vomiting (Dragonfly in Amber, chapter 8).

When it comes to growing Wood Betony, you will first need to understand that it is part of the mint family. What this means is that this plant is not hard to identify. It has a square stem that is covered in white hairs along with spear shaped leaves. This herbaceous perennial grows to a height of 12 inches prior to blooming. In the summer, this herb will produce 2 to 3 foot stems that are topped with reddish-purple blooms.

Wood betony is propagated by seed, division, and cuttings. Since most people do not know whether they have wood betony in their garden, seed propagation will be covered.

To begin the seed propagation process, starts off with exposing your seeds to the cold. The easiest way of doing this is to fill a small resealable bag with vermiculite or potting soil. Once that is done, add a little water to the planting medium and work it around. After the planting medium is evenly moistened, add the seeds and seal the bag up. Place the bag in the refrigerator for 21 days.

About 20 days into the cold process, you will need to clean and sterilize your pot of choice. The only exception to this is if you are using peat pots. Once the container has been sterilized, allow it to dry. Fill the dried container with a good all-purpose potting soil. Remove the bag from the refrigerator and sprinkle the seed and soil on top of the container's soil surface. Water the soil until moisture can be seen coming out the bottom of the container. Place the planted container in a sunny location and in 7 to 14 days you will see evidence of seed germination. Continue to take care of the seedling until your local frost-free date has arrived. At this point, you are ready to plant your seedlings in the ground but harden them off first.

Wood betony loves to be planted in full sun to partial shade. When it comes to spacing, this herb grows best when you plant it so that there is 10 to 12 inches between each plant.

If you do not want to get a jump on the gardening season, plan on planting wood betony seeds during the late summer, fall, and/or early spring. Planting during these times will still meet the cold exposure requirement.

To keep this herb looking its best, divide the plant every 3 to four years. This will prevent the crown of the plant from dying off.

BISTORT

Persicaria bistorta

This is another herb that can be found with several different names. In the past, it was named *Polygonum bistorta.* Today, it can be found under the previous name alongside *Persicaria bistorta, Bristorta amplexicaulis* or knotweed. In medieval times, bistort was actually called persicaria, which actually came from a Latin term "*persica*." This latter term means "peach." While you may think that it is referring to a fruit, this term was actually describing the leaf shape. During ancient times, the term "peach" was referred to as "*persike*" or "*persica*." This new term no longer described a leaf shape; instead it described an area by which the "Persian Apple" came from. In this example, it described a fruit that came from Persia, went through China, and arrived in Europe.

Another interesting note about this plant is why it is commonly called knotweed. This name starts off with the term "bistort," which in Latin means twice twisted. To make communication easy for those who did not know Latin, the common name simply described the natural growth habit of "bistort."

In the past, this herb was used to stop bleeding, treat ulcers, jaundice, and even for the treatment of diabetes. Due to bistort's multiple uses, this is why Claire wanted it for her medical kit for her trip to the West Indies in search of Ian (Voyager, chapter 40).

When it comes to growing your own bistort, there are a few things you need to know. First, this herb is a semi-evergreen perennial that can be grown in USDA Plant Hardiness Zones 4 through 9. This plant loves to be grown in full sun locations but can take some shade. The soil needs to be moist and well-draining. To get the most out of your bistort, add compost to the soil when you first plant.

Now that you know the general requirements, let's talk about a negative. The moist soil conditions that were described previously are easily found around ponds. When bistort is planted around ponds, it becomes an invasive species. In doing so, pick your planting location carefully.

When it comes to propagating this herb, it can be started by seed or division. Seed propagation can be started indoors or outside. Starting your bistort inside should occur early in spring. The process begins by cleaning and sterilizing the container. Once that is done, simply sprinkle the seed on the soil surface and cover with a slight layer of soil. Water the seeds from the bottom and place the planted container on a sunny windowsill in a room that is kept between 65 and 75 degrees Fahrenheit. Check the soil often and water when the soil feels slightly dry. Germination will take 3 to 4 weeks.

If you do not want to start your bistort's seeds indoors but want to get a jump on the season, consider planting your seeds in a cold frame in the spring. When using this approach, allow the seedlings to remain in the cold frame until they are a size that you can handle without causing damage. Once they have reached that size, transplant them into individual pots and care for them until summer or they are large enough to plant in the garden space.

If the seedlings are still small, you can overwinter them in their pots in a cold frame.

Direct seeding into the garden is another choice. This can occur after your local frost-free date or in the late summer. The general process is the same but you will need to diligent when it comes to soil moisture. Make sure that the garden's soil is moist but not dripping wet at all times. If you allow the soil to dry out during the seed germination process, you will lose your seedlings.

The last propagation technique is through division. What makes division work for this herb is its rhizomes. These same rhizomes are what also can make it invasive.

When it comes to dividing this plant, you will simply need to dig it up and cut the rhizome into pieces making sure you have some leaves attached.

Regardless of your propagation method, you will need to space the plants three feet apart.

BLADDERWORT

Utricularia macrohiza

Bladderworts are plants that can be found all over the world and in the Northern Hemisphere, this plant grows in all 50 states. This plant can be divided into three types based on where they grow. This includes terrestrial, epiphytic, and aquatic. The general characteristic of this plant is the "bladder," which is also indicated in its name. The Latin term *Utricularia* can be translated to mean "little bag."

The general structure of this plant consists of a stem like root system that exists in the planting medium. From these structures, you will see the "bladders," which when open will catch food for the plant. Finally, the top of the plant is why many people grow bladderworts and that is for the blooms.

When it comes to propagating bladderworts, you can either start them from seed or division. Depending on the type of bladderwort you plan to grow will determine the amount of submersion in water your plant will have to be under. But, regardless of which type, the soil needs to always remain moist.

To start your bladderwort from seed begins with cleaning the container and sterilizing it. Once that is done, you will need to make up the planting medium for your seeds. Bladderwort planting medium consists of 1 part sand to 1 part peat moss. Mix this mixture thoroughly and place in the sterilized pot. If you have a friend with a bladderwort, you can harvest the seeds easily from the blooms. This ease of seed harvesting is why some domesticated bladderworts can be considered weeds in indoor gardening environments.

Once you have your seeds, you may notice something. They are very small and since they are small you will only need to sprinkle them on the soil's surface. Next, place the planted pot on a tray and add ½ to 1 inch of water to the tray. Keeping this amount in the tray at all times will provide the consistent moisture that this plant requires.

The second way of propagating the bladderwort is through cutting a piece of the stem like root system. Oncc that is done, repot in the planting medium described previously.

Once you have propagated your bladderwort, put it in a location that receives at least 4 or more hours of direct sunlight.

While terrestrial bladderworts feed themselves through attracting soil nematodes to their bladders, aquatic bladderworts will need to be feed. The easiest way to do this is to submerge the plant in pond water several times so that the plant can trap its own food. If you are growing an epiphyte bladderwort, mist it with a diluted amount of epiphytic orchard fertilizer once a month from spring to fall. This dilution should be ¼ teaspoon per gallon of filtered water.

If you do not want to utilize the tray with water method, consider growing epiphyte and aquatic bladderworts in vented terrariums or aquariums. When using this approach, make sure that the container is vented and place the container under a 40 watt fluorescent light that is suspend six inches above the container. Let this light remain on for 14 hours a day during the spring and summer. Shorten the amount of sunlight to only 12 hours a day during the fall and winter months.

In the past, bladderwort was used to make a tea that treated such ailments as urinary tract infections, kidney stones, and even for weight loss. It was applied to the skin as a way of reducing inflammation from burns.

Claire mentions that bladderwort can be used to treat systemic infections (Voyager, chapter 40). While the symptoms described above indicate that it could be used for systemic infections, there is no evidence as to how or if this works.

BLOODWORT

Sanguinaria canadensis

Bloodwort is just one of the names for *Sanguinaria Canadensis.* Other names include blood root, red root, and Indian red paint. As you may have noticed, there seems to be a theme going on when it comes to this plant and that is the color red. This theme comes from the fact that if the stems or roots are cut in two they bleed red. This red color looks like blood and in doing so contributes to the name. To take advantage of this red sap, many ancient people used this sap to make red, pink, and even orange dye. While this is a viable use for the sap, make sure to wear gloves when handling bloodwort. It is known to cause skin irritation that is equivalent to poison ivy.

When it comes to growing your own bloodwort, you are in for a treat. This plant fits right into a woodland landscape or shady garden space. Do not have either one of these environments? Do not fret; bloodwort can even be grown in a container.

Bloodwort's height can reach to just less than six inches but has a spread of 12 inches, which makes it perfect as a ground cover. This perennial easily grows in USDA Plant Hardiness Zones 3 through 9. When growing bloodwort, there are only two requirements. One the soil needs to be moist while well-draining and they prefer partially sunny to shady locations.

Propagating bloodwort is not difficult at all. If you have a friend that already has bloodwort, you can simply harvest some seeds in the early spring or divide the plant.

Prior to working with bloodwort, always wear gloves.

When it comes to harvesting the seeds, you will first need to know a little about the life cycle of bloodwort. This plant is one of the first plants that bloom in early spring. In mid to late spring, you will begin to see seedpods. Once this happens, harvest them and place them in a paper bag. Shake the bag so that the seeds are released from the pods. The next step of this process is to prepare the ground. Remove any unwanted plant material and mix in one to two inches of well seasoned compost. What you are actually doing is mimicking a woodland environment. While you may have picked a partially shady to shady location, a trick to planting bloodwort is to place it under a deciduous tree. In the early spring the sun is not that bright and the blooming of this plant can occur with the fear of scorching. When the sun's rays get stronger, the leaves of the deciduous tree have leafed out. This, in turn, provides more shade and prevents the emerald green leaves from burning.

After the garden space has been prepared, sprinkle the seeds on the soil's surface. Water the seeds in and keep the soil moist.

When it comes to digging up a start of bloodwort, this can really be done anytime. Since this plant spreads by rhizomes, what you really are digging up is rhizomes. Once you have your rhizomes removed from the mother plant, move them to their new location. The hole size needs to be slightly wider than the rhizome and 4 inches deep. Place the rhizome in the hole so that it is near the soil surface. Fill in as needed with well seasoned compost. To help control weeds and mimic leaf litter, add a one to two inch layer of bark mulch.

Water in the rhizome and continue to water twice a week during the spring and summer months. This will keep the plant from going dormant.

In the past, bloodwort was used in dentistry as a way of treating plaque buildup. It has been also used to treat sore throats, aching joints, to cause vomiting, and as a cancer treatment. As far as Geillis telling Claire that bloodwort would remove a wart (Outlander only, chapter 9), it is mentioned that wart removal was another use for this herb.

BOGBEAN

Menyanthes trifoliate

The bogbean is an aquatic plant that can survive in water that is 12 inches deep. In doing so, this plant works well in a bog landscape design or pond. It does not do well in shady locations and prefers the sun. The plant itself can become invasive due to the fact that it grows fro rhizomes. As these rhizomes spread the large, three lobbed, dark green leaves can be seen floating. During the spring and summer, the foliage will be topped with white flowers that resemble stars.

While you can propagate the bogbean from seed, the easier route is to purchase divisions or cuttings. Before you do make the purchase, make sure that this plant is not on your state's invasive species list even if you live in its USDA Plant Hardiness Zones 3 through 7.

Yes, you can harvest your own rhizomes in the spring if you know someone who has bogbean growing in their pond or bog. If you decide to go this route, do not harvest from small clumps. Larger groupings will need to be divided any way so take advantage of this fact. Plus harvesting from larger clumps will make it more likely that you will dig up a rhizome with at least one growing tip.

Once you have your bogbean rhizomes, the planting process is simple. What you will need to do is to just plant the rhizome in the mud around the edge of a pond or bog. Space the rhizomes so that there is 8 to 12 inches between each rhizome. If the bogbean has been planted in a pond, the moisture level of the soil is not an issue. On the other hand, a bog can sometime dry out. If you planted your bogbean in a bog, check the soil moisture often and water as needed.

Once you get bogbean established, it pretty much takes care of itself. To encourage the plant to bloom more, remove any spent blooms or deadhead.

Bogbean has been used to treat aching joints, upset stomach, and even as a way of increasing one's appetite. It is also noted, that this herb was used to treat fevers, which is what Claire used bogbean for while she was at the Abbey of the Ste. Anne de Beaupre (Cross Stitch only, chapter 39).

BONESET

Eupatorium perfoliatum

Boneset is a hardy perennial that can be found by other names, which includes white snakeroot, mist flower, feverwort and Joe Pye weed. The common name boneset comes from the fact that it was used to treat "break bone fever." Beyond using this herb as a fever reducer in the past, it has also been used as to treat colds, constipation, and just a general cure all.

This herb can be found growing in USDA Plant Hardiness Zones 3 through 9. The unique white flowers of the plant appear during the mid summer and continue well into the fall. If you are looking to incorporate this plant into your landscaping, consider using it in a wildflower patch or as a backdrop to a perennial garden since this plant can reach the mature height of 4 feet.

When it comes to growing boneset, you will first need to find the best location. This plant requires a moist but well-draining soil that has a pH between 5.8 and 6.8. If you are really not sure as to whether the soil is moist enough, consider planting your boneset in a depression. This is a good location for moist soil as long as it is not standing in water.

As far as the sunlight requirement of this plant, it is flexible. It will grow in full sun to partial shade.

Propagation of boneset is through seed. The seed can either be directly seeded into the garden space in late summer to early fall. If using this technique, do not expect to see any germination of the seed. The reason for this is the fact that the seed needs to be exposed to the cold before seed germination will occur.

If you want to get a jump on the gardening season then you will need to start your seeds indoors. To begin this process, you will need to pull your calendar out and count back 3 weeks from your local frost-free date. This is the date by which you can start your seed but do not jump into the planting process. These seeds will need to be cold stratified. When it comes to exposing these seeds to the cold, you will first need to place some potting soil in a bowl and moisten evenly with water. Keep in mind though that you want the soil moist but not dripping wet. Once you have prepared the soil, place it in a zip up type plastic bag, and place your seed in the bag. Mix the soil and seeds together and seal. Place the plastic bag in the refrigerator for 30 days prior to your planting date.

Monitor the soil moisture in the bag and remove any seeds that have germinated. Plant these seedlings in a container, put on a sunny windowsill, and continue to check the soil moisture.

After the seeds have gone through their 30 day cold exposure, take the bag to the planned garden space. Gently disperse the soil and seeds.

Boneset seeds require sunlight to germinate so only cover with a slight layer of soil. Mist with water using a misting bottle and in 7 to 14 days you will begin to see signs of seed germination. Continue to monitor soil moisture until the seedlings are well established.

Once the seedlings are large enough to handle, thin them out so that there is 8 to 12 inches between each plant. If you are a frugal gardener, you can gently remove the unwanted seedlings and plant them elsewhere. On the other hand, if you simply want to thin them out take a pair of scissors and cut away the surplus seedlings.

Boneset is a prolific seed producer and if the seeds drop, you will have new plant additions. To prevent the boneset from spreading to unwanted areas, remove the spent flowers before they go to seed.

As stated before, boneset was used as a tea or tincture whenever the symptoms of flu or cold would appear. This was noted when a boneset tea was made in the storyline (Outlander only, chapter 4).

BORAGE

Borago officialis

Borage is a beautiful annual plant that produces stems and leaves that are covered in coarse hairs. The stems themselves are topped with blooms that are star shaped and sky-blue color. While the common name for this herb is borage, old herbalists refer to this as bugloss.

There is some confusion as to where the name borage actually came from. Some believe that the Latin term "borage" actually came from corage, which can be translated as "cor" or "from the heart" and ago otherwise means "I bring." Other authorities say the term comes from the Mediterranean where the Italian *borra,* Low Latin *burra,* and French *bourra* can be translated to mean flock, hair or wool. Any of these terms describe the hairs that grow along the stem and leaves. The final translation comes from the Celtic term *barrach,* which means "man of courage." Since there is no clear evidence as to where this name came from, it still up for debate.

In the wild, this plant loves disturbed areas and fits quite easily in a kitchen garden. The best part is the fact that this herb is well known to attract beneficial insects, which includes bees. One of the byproducts of having borage growing in your garden space is the delicious honey that is produced by the visiting honeybees.

As far as growing borage goes, the first thing you need to do is to pick the proper location. Borage requires partial shade to full sun. It also needs a loose, well-draining soil that has a pH of 6.6. Beyond these requirements, the only other issues that one needs to consider is the height and self- sowing. Borage will reach two to three feet in height once it matures. It will also self- seed so plan on an area that is only going to be used for borage.

If you do not want to worry about borage popping up in unwanted spaces, consider planting it in a container.

Borage is propagated by seed. When it comes to planting it, the best approach is to directly seed it into your garden space since it does not transplant well. To begin this process, you will need to prepare the soil by removing any unwanted plant material. Loosen the soil down six inches and incorporate a good amount of well-seasoned compost. Once that is done, you are ready to plant after your local frost-free date.

When it comes to planting the seed, simply lay down a ruler and place one seed per 12 inches. Cover with less than 1/8 inch of soil and water in. While the spacing may seem extreme, the plant size warrants it and growing the borage in clumps will allow the plants to support themselves. On the other hand, if you do not want to measure the space off then simply broadcast and thin after the seedlings have received their second set of leaves.

Continue to monitor soil moisture throughout the plants' life. To get the most out of your borage, consider planting around your strawberries. It is said that borage increase the yield of strawberries.

When it comes to the uses for borage, the leaves, stems, and the oil from the seed is all used. The borage seed oil is used as a treatment for skin disorders along with stress, inflammation, and even heart disease. The flowers and leaves are used to treat coughs, and fevers. A noted unique use for borage is increasing milk production in lactating women. All these uses may be why Claire noted that borage was growing in the gardens at Leoch (Outlander, chapter 24). Bugloss was one of the herbs added to Claire's list of supplies she wanted for her medical kit when her and Jamie were going to travel to the West Indies in search of Ian (Voyager, chapter 40).

BURDOCK

Arctium lappa

Burdock or Gobo is normally viewed as a weed in USDA Plant Hardiness Zones 2 through 10. It can be found growing along waterways in areas that receive dabbles of shade to full sun. This plant is considered a biennial and easily reseeds itself, which can make it a problem in many gardens.

This herb is propagated through seeds that can be planted either in fall after your last killing frost, or indoors 4 weeks prior to your local frost-free date. Since this plant easily germinates from seed, I would recommend directly seeding into the garden. The reason for this is two-fold. First, the seeds germinating are not a problem and second, planting the seeds in the fall will naturally expose them to the cold, which is required for proper seed germination.

When it comes to planting the seeds outdoors, the first step of this process consists of selecting the proper site and preparing the garden space. A sunny location is ideal with a well-draining to sandy soil. Once you have found the location, remove any unwanted plant material, smooth the soil surface and sprinkle the seeds on top. Add ¼ inch of soil on top of the seeds and water in. Keep the soil evenly moist and in 7 to 14 days, you will begin to see evidence of seed germination. Continue to water as needed until the burdock becomes established in the garden.

An interesting note about this six-foot tall plant is its role in the development of Velcro. During the second year, the burdock will produce a flower stalk that is topped with a purple bloom. From this bloom, seeds will be produced that have a bur on them. This bur and their ability to "cling" to things is where the idea for Velcro came about.

When it comes to the uses for burdock, this plant has been used in the past as a wrap by which you could steam food in. This was purpose that Jamie wrapped the trout in burdock leaves (Outlander only, chapter 16). Clair also used burdock as a way of reducing a fever while at the Abbey of Ste. Anne de Beaupre (Cross Stitch only, chapter 39).

In actuality, this plant has been used for the above uses along with treating other ailments, which includes dry skin, increasing sex drive, and liver disease. It has also been used as a treatment for "arteriosclerosis" or hardening of the arteries.

BUTTERBUR

Petasites hybridus or Petasites japonicas

Depending on where you live, you will either have *Petasites hybridus* or *Petasites japonicas.* The *Petasites hybridus* can be found growing along pond banks in Europe and Asia. *Petasites japonicas* can only be found in Japan, or in areas where Japanese migrated. When referring to butterbur, it is assumed that the *Petasites hybridus* is the one that is discussed. Assuming this, butterbur also goes by sweet coltsfoot or pestilence wort.

When it comes to growing this plant, location is everything. Butterbur grows best in full sun and in a soil that is deeply fertile with a lot of humus. It can be found growing wild in USDA Plant Hardiness Zones 4 through 8.

Propagating butterbur can occur through seed or division. When it comes to growing butterbur from seed, you will first need to start the seed in a cold frame. Since this plant's seed loses vitality quickly, you will want to plant the seed as soon as it has ripened in the spring. Once the seeds have been harvested, simply sprinkle the seed on the soil's surface in the cold frame. Cover with less than 1/8 inch of soil. Water the seed and never let the soil dry out.

As soon as the seedlings are big enough to handle, transplant them into individual pots. Once the summer season arrives, move the seedlings to their permanent location.

The second form of propagation is division. This can be done from spring to early fall. The process is simple and only requires you to dig up part of the butterbur plant making sure that your division has some root. Replant the division in the new location.

This plant can become a pest due to the fact that it can spread by root and seed. To keep it from spreading, consider planting your butterbur in a pot and then burying the pot in the ground. This will keep the runners under control. When it comes to seed production, only grow male plants. The butterbur plant is dioecious, which means that the male and female plants are different. But, if your goal is seed production, make sure that the male and female plants are placed close together.

While this plant is only referred to by Claire as growing near the millpond close to Lallybroch (Cross Stitch only, chapter 28), it has been used in the medical field in the past. It has been used to treat a wide range of problems, which include urinary tract spasms, pain, upset stomach, and even as a way of stimulating the appetite. When applied to the skin, it has also been used as a way of speeding up the healing process of wounds.

CAMOMILE

Chamaemelum nobile or Matricaria recutita

While you may feel that this herb is misspelled, the spelling above is the British version. This spelling is used in Cross Stitch. The alternative spelling is chamomile but in this section the British spelling will be used.

The reason for the two Latin names is the fact that camomile comes in two types. This includes Roman chamomile (*Chamaemelum nobile)*, which is also referred to as Russian or English and German *(Matricaria recutita)*. The Roman camomile is perennial low growing form of camomile that resembles a green mat with daisy like flowers. The German variety has the same look as the Roman but grows one to two feet erect. While both camomiles are viewed as a perennial, only the Roman type truly can be called a perennial. Due to the reseeding nature of the German, it is still viewed an annual.

If you want to grow chamomile outside as a "perennial," you will need to live in USDA Plant Hardiness Zones 3 through 9.

The choices of propagation for this herb include seed, and division. Seed propagation will be covered but for directions on plant division, check out the garden primer.

Planting chamomile seed starts off with planning. If you live in one of the hardiness zones noted above then you can plant your seed in the fall or spring. For those individuals who do not live in these locations, you will need to grow your seed indoors first in the spring.

The first step in this process is preparing your container as described in the garden primer. Once cleaned and sterilized, fill the container with a well-draining potting medium that is moist. Next, sprinkle your seeds on top. Camomile seeds require sunlight to germinate. In doing so, do not cover the seeds with soil. Mist the soil surface to moisten the seeds and settle them to the soil surface.

Place your planted container on a sunny windowsill and continue to check the soil moisture. In 7 to 14 days, you will see signs that your seeds have germinated.

Once the seedlings have their second set of leaves and are large enough to handle, transplant into individual pots.

Two weeks prior to your local frost-free date, harden off your seedlings. Plant your camomile in an area that receives partial shade. If that is not possible, it can grow in full sun. When it comes to the soil requirement, this herb is not picky but it does require a well-draining soil. To keep your chamomile looking its best, plant your seedlings with six inches between them.

Need a year round supply of chamomile? Well, you can easily grow it as part of an indoor herb garden. If you choose this path, remember how large this herb can get and pick your container accordingly.

Camomile is a wonderful herb and as a companion can help out both vegetables and other herbs. But if your camomile becomes weak, it will attract garden pests such as aphids, mealybugs and/or thrips. To reduce the chances of this happening, monitor the soil moisture and water when needed. Also, do not fertilize this plant. This will produce leaves that have a weak scent and flower production will be down.

When this herb is planted outside, it can easily take over in no time. Control is essential and this is especially true when it comes to the German variety. To reduce reseeding, remove the spent flowers.

One of the common uses for camomile is to take the leaves and steep them with water to make a tea with calming properties (Cross Stitch only, chapter 4), and (Outlander, chapter 38). A suggestion is made by Claire to Ian senior to rub some camomile lotion on his stump when it ached (Cross Stitch only, chapter 26).

Camomile plus other herbs were combined to make a calming tonic for Margaret Campbell (Voyager, chapter 29). Due to the calming effects this herb has, Claire felt it was important enough to put it on the list of herbs she needed for her medical kit that she planned on taking with her on the voyage to the West Indies in search of Ian (Voyager, chapter 40).

When one hears the name camomile, the first thought is tea. Many people drink camomile tea to help them sleep but there are other uses.

This herb has been used as a treatment for such things as digestive system disorders, hay fever, and even menstrual cramps. Some individuals inhale the steam from steeping camomile to treat certain respiratory ailments, such as swelling and irritation of the lungs. Applying this herb as a compress to the skin can help give relief to hemorrhoids, and sore nipples from nursing. It has also been used as preventative measure when it comes to chemotherapy and radiation. Simply wiping the inside of the mouth with this herb helps with treating and/or preventing the damage to the skin that can be caused by these modern treatments.

CARAWAY

Carum carvi

Believe it or not, some experts consider caraway one of the oldest condiments. It has been used in Eastern European dishes along with a key ingredient in love potions. The reason why caraway was used in love potions is the belief that caraway could never be stolen. In doing so, a love potion made with caraway and given as a gift would forever preserve that love. Livestock were also given caraway seed as part of their feed. The reason for this was the belief that anything containing caraway seed could not be stolen; hence the livestock would be protected from thieves.

Caraway shares a family (Angelica) with other edibles, which include carrot, and dill. All these plants share a unique bloom. This bloom is umbel-shaped, which allows the tiny white flowers to be displayed on top. Once the flowers are spent, seeds will form and can be harvested by simply cutting the blooms, placing them upside down in a paper bag, and hanging up in a cool but dry location. As the seeds dry, they will fall into the paper bag.

Caraway requires full sun but can tolerate partial shade. The soil needs to be well-draining but full of organic matter. To meet this requirement, add a good amount of well seasoned compost or manure.

This herb is a biennial and thrives in USDA Plant Hardiness Zones 3 through 9. While you can directly seed into the prepared garden, if you live in USDA Plant Hardiness Zones 3 through 6, you may want to start your seeds indoors four to six weeks prior to your local frost-free date. In other areas, simply plant the seed after your local frost-free date.

Planting caraway in the herb garden is easy and starts off with preparing the garden site. Once that is done, pull out your ruler and measure off increments of eight inches. Mark these areas with powdered milk. This is the proper spacing of caraway but if you do not want to do this, simply sprinkle your seed on the soil surface and cover with ¼ inch of soil. Mist the soil and keep it evenly moist. You should expect to see signs of seed germination in 8 to 12 days. At that point, thin out the seedlings so that there is eight inches between each plant.

While caraway does well in the herb garden, you can plant it in a container that is 12 to 14 inches in diameter and 10 inches deep. Clean and sterilize your chosen pot, add drainage material, fill with a mixture of equal parts of well-seasoned compost and all-purpose potting soil. Water the soil in and then plant two seeds. Why just two seeds? Well, caraway needs room and can grow to a height of two feet. Two seeds can be started but the weakest seedling will need to be removed.

Place your potted caraway plant outside during the summer in a sunny location. When you bring it indoors, place it in a cool room that receives a lot of direct sunlight.

If you keep your caraway indoors all the time, do not expect to get any seed but you can enjoy the foliage in dishes.

Some individuals find that chilling the seed in the freezer for a few days improves the germination rate of caraway.

Beyond using caraway seed and leaves in dishes, consuming caraway seed can be used to treat all sorts of digestive problems. These problems include loss of appetite, bloating, and even heartburn. Claire jokes with Jamie when she tells him that Master Raymond would pierce her nipples in exchange for her caraway tonic recipe (Dragonfly in Amber, chapter 9).

Caraway oil is used to treat coughs by which you want to bring up phlegm. It also kills bacteria in the body, increases urination, and relieves constipation. Women have been known to use caraway oil to bring forth menstruation, treat cramps and increase milk production. When rubbed on the skin, caraway oil can improve skin circulation.

CARDAMOM

Elettaria cardamomum

This herb is commonly grown in the tropics of Guatemala, India, and Vietnam. But, believe it or not, you can have some success in USDA Plant Hardiness Zones 10 through 13. While you can grow it indoors, the mature size of this tree is 10 feet or more.

When it comes to the cardamom, you are faced with two types. This includes the green and black, but regardless of which type of cardamom you may want to grow, this herb can be challenge.

Why is this? Well, beyond the environmental conditions, cardamom seeds typically have a poor germination rate. Some speculate that the reason for this is the hard coat on the seed. To improve the chances of germination, one will need to treat the seed coat. This treatment will soften up the coat so that the seedling can emerge. While there are several ways one can do this, the safest is to rough up the seed coat with sandpaper, then nick the seed coat in a few areas with a knife. The goal is to mimic the damage that would be done if an animal chewed on it.

Please note: there are other sources that do not mention this step but this seed treatment makes sense. The seed coat of this herb is hard and mimicking nature is a great way of improving germination rates. Also, realize that whole cardamom sold in stores will not germinate. Commercially grown cardamom is picked early. This early selection does not allow the seed to ripen.

After you have prepared your seed, the next step is to prepare your container by cleaning and sterilizing it. Once that is done, put drainage material in the bottom and fill with a potting soil that mixed with well seasoned compost. Water the soil until you see moisture coming out the bottom of the container. Plant the seeds 1/8 inch down into the soil. Lightly cover with soil and mist. Put your planted container in a room that is kept between 72 to 80 degrees Fahrenheit. Keep the container away from direct sunlight.

Water your planted pot daily and mist the soil surface. In 14 days, hopefully you will see your seedlings breaking ground.

Once your seeds have germinated, continue to monitor the soil moisture and never let the soil dry out. Also, do not allow the room's temperature fluctuate and only permit a few hours a day of filtered sunlight.

Feed your cardamom tree every two weeks with a fertilizer that is high in phosphorus, and potassium. This should only be done during the growing season.

The value of this plant as a culinary herb is timeless. It was no problem for Claire to bribe the cook on the Arternis, Mr. Murphy, with this and other spices (Voyager, chapter 41).

CASCARA

Rhamnus purshiana, Cascara sagrada or Frangula purshiana

As you may note, cascara has several Latin names and more common names. These include cascara buckthorn, bitter cascara, sacred bark, mountain cranberry bark, and bitter bark just to name a few. This evergreen shrub or tree is native to western North America and British Columbia but if you live in this area, do not run to the nursery for your cascara. You will not find any of the propagation methods available for sell in the United States. Your best solution to this problem is to find a friend who has one and will give you seed and/or cuttings. If you live in Europe, it is easier to find this plant and it will thrive in UK Plant Hardiness Zone up to 7.

This plant has been used by many different groups of people in the past. In California, priests actually gave it the name *Cascara sagrada,* which means sacred bark. This translation can be taken in two ways. Some believe it refers to the medical uses of the bark. Others feel that the name is derived from the fact that bark resembles the wood that was used to build the Ark of the Covenant. The wood was used to make chisel handles by the Nuu-chah-nulth people. The Skagit people also made a green dye from the bark. Other Native People collected the fresh bark and dried it to make a medicine to treat constipation. This plant material was used in constipation medication in the United States until 2002. At this point, the FDA required proof that the cascara was safe to use. Drug companies felt the tests were too expensive and did not comply. In doing so, the use of cascara as an ingredient in constipation medication was prohibited in 2002.

While cascara is not used in over-the-counter laxative treatments in the United States, an interesting fact still remains. In the past, only the fresh bark was harvested. Depending on how the bark was harvested, this would kill the tree. But, it was discovered that the wood contained 50 percent of the active ingredient. Once that was discovered, cascara trees began to fall. To protect them, laws were established to prevent overharvesting. After a synthetic version was created, the law was withdrawn.

Believe it or not, the bark and/or wood are not the only sources of the active ingredient. Bees visiting the cascara blooms will produce a honey that also has a mild laxative effect.

Beyond being used as a laxative, cascara is used in the treatment of gallstones, and liver problems. In the food industry, the bitterness of cascara is used to flavor food.

In the Outlander book series and STARZ show, bitter cascara is mentioned several times. Master Raymond makes up "pretend" poison for his clients (Dragonfly in Amber, chapter 8). When the Comte St Germain goes to Master Raymond, he purchases some "poison" by which he gives to Claire (Dragonfly in Amber, chapter 16). Bitter cascara is used again but in this situation Claire is looking for herbs that will help her mimic the symptoms of smallpox (Dragonfly in Amber, chapter 23). The reason Claire ponders on using this herb is the fact that discomfort and diarrhea are common symptoms of smallpox.

When propagating cascara, it can be started from seed or cuttings. If you are lucky enough to find a source by which you can purchase, chances are you will find bare rooted, and container-grown specimens. Since most gardeners will choose one of these types of sources, environmental conditions will only be discussed. Check the garden primer for details on how to plant bare-rooted and container-grown specimens.

Picking the right location for this plant is really going to come down to finding enough space. The mature height of this tree is 32 feet with the width being 19 feet. The soil type is really not important for this plant but what is important is the fact that the soil is well-draining while remaining moist. This requirement is a little confusing but take a walk along a stream and notice the soil, which is moist and well-draining. The only true requirement that the cascara is really picky about is sunlight. It can tolerate some partial shade but if possible plant in full sun.

CATNIP

Nepeta cataria

This hardy perennial herb is not only known as catnip but also as catmint. While the common names come from the fact that cats love to roll and nibble on this plant, the genus name came from a Roman town. During this time period, Nepeti was where catnip production occurred.

Beyond growing this plant for your cats, there are many other uses for this herb. In the past, it was dried and smoked to reduce stress. When the leaves are used fresh, they can treat upset stomachs, reduce fevers, and even calm a headache. Claire took advantage of the fever reducing properties of this herb when she used it while at the Abbey of Ste. Anne de Beaupre (Outlander, chapter 39). The most unique use for this herb is as a meat tenderizer.

When it comes to propagating catnip, you have several different choices. This includes seed, division, and stem cuttings.

As far as starting your seeds indoors, this can easily be done for indoor enjoyment or to get a jump on the gardening season. When using this technique, make sure to only put your plants out after your local frost-free date.

Another approach is to plant the seed in rows during the late fall or early spring. The key to planting the seed is to just sprinkle it on top of the soil and cover with less than ¼ inch. When conditions are right, the seeds will germinate naturally outdoors.

Once your seedlings have reached five-inches in height, thin them out so that there is 12 to 18 inches between each plant but do not just pull them out. The best approach is to simply take a pair of scissors and cut away the unwanted plants.

Catnip really has only a few growing requirements. First, it is hardy in USDA Plant Hardiness Zones 3a through 9b. It also requires a sunny location that receives at least eight to 10 hours of bright sunlight. The soil needs to be well-draining and loose.

While you may have seen Common Catnip that grows to three feet in height, has grayish-green leaves and white flowers, there are three other varieties that you may not be familiar with. This includes Camphor Catnip, which is one you need to grow if you want to keep cats away due to the camphor smell. The other characteristic of this catnip is the fact that it is a shorter variety. Lemon Catnip looks a lot like Common Catnip but the difference can be seen in the flower. While the flower of the Lemon Catnip is white the difference can be seen by a simple purple spot. The other difference can be smelled. As the name applies, Lemon Catnip smells like lemons. The last variety is called Greek Catnip, which only reaches 18 inches in height at maturity, has light green leaves, and pink flowers.

To keep this herb looking its best, pinch off the flowers to encourage the plant to grow bushy.

CHELIDONIUM

Chelidonium majus

While not all plants brought to the United States by the Europeans became pests, chelidonium or greater celandine is one labeled an invasive species. It can be found growing wild in USDA Plant Hardiness Zones 5 through 8.

The uses for this herb are numerous and include the treatment of digestive tract issues, detoxification, gout, and even arteriosclerosis. It is also used to treat liver and gallbladder problems. In the story, Davie Beaton takes greater celandine as a treatment for his jaundice (Outlander, chapter 7).

Pain treatment is another use for this herb, which includes tooth and menstrual. This use may be the reason why Master Raymond gave Claire the greater celandine for Mary Hawkins (Dragonfly in Amber, chapter 20). While it is noted that it was to induce sleep, a reduction in pain will help a person sleep and in doing so would have aided Mary Hawkins in slumber.

When it comes to growing greater celandine, please check with your local extension agent for invasiveness of this plant in your area.

If you decide to grow this plant, it really is not picky and will survive in any soil type that is well-draining and rich in organic matter. Your plant also needs to be in at least in partial shade to full coverage.

The only way to propagate this short lived perennial is through planting seed but this seed can take up to 12 months to germinate. At this point, you can decide to directly seed into the garden space in the spring or fall. While this would space, it will not save your time. During the period that you would be waiting for the seeds to germinate, you will need to be diligent on your weed control. What this means is a lot of pulling weeds by hand. Another approach is to prepare a flat and fill it with a good soil. Moisten the soil and sprinkle your seeds on top. Mist with water and place in a location that is partially shady. Check the soil moisture and water as needed. As the seeds germinate and become large enough to handle, transplant into individual pots or directly into the garden space.

To reduce the chances of your greater celandine spreading, pull up the plant material as soon as the plant has bloomed.

CHICKWEED

Stellaria media

If you own a lawn, you are very familiar with chickweed as a stubborn weed. While it is classified as an annual, the fact that it reseeds so easily makes some individuals believe it is a perennial. Chickweed likes a slightly moist soil that is located in an area that receives dapples of sunlight or light shade.

While you can grow your chickweed indoor, planting this weed in your garden is just as easy. In doing so, the container version will be described just to keep the chickweed from popping up in your yard.

To begin the process, first prepare your container by cleaning it. For details on this process, check out the garden primer. Once it has been cleaned, place drainage material in the bottom. Next, make a rich soil for your chickweed by creating a 50:50 mix of all-purpose potting soil and well seasoned compost. Yes, I know that chickweed is not picky about its soil requirement, if you are going to eat it you want to create the best environment. In this case, this plant needs a well-draining soil that is rich in organic material.

After the soil mixture has been combined, moisten the soil and fill your container to an inch from the top. Go out and harvest some chickweed from your yard or a friend's yard. I promise you they will let you have all you want. Next, sprinkle the seeds on top and cover with ¼ inch of soil. Mist the soil surface with water. Move your chickweed to a shady area. Continue to monitor soil moisture.

Thin your chickweed seedlings out once they are three inches in height. Give your chickweed plants a haircut often to keep the plant looking its best.

Uses for this herb go beyond an edible green. Eaten, it can be used to treat scurvy, blood disorders, and lung problems, such as asthma. When applied to the skin, it can help reduce muscle, and joint pain along with boils, and itching of the skin.

When Claire received lashes on her back at the witch trial, Jamie chewed chickweed and then applied it to her back (Cross Stitch only, chapter 25). This application occurred for several reasons. One was for the pain relief. The second reason could be for the vitamin C content, which would have been released when Jamie chewed it. This latter is just speculation.

Cinquefoil

Potentilla reptans

Cinquefoil grows in USDA Plant Hardiness Zones 2 through 7. The cinquefoil name includes a grass-like plant and deciduous shrubs. Regardless of the growth type, cinquefoils cover themselves in yellow or pink buttercup shaped blooms in June and to produce these blooms until fall. The cinquefoil is a wonderful addition to a butterfly garden for two reasons. One, it is deer tolerant and two, it is a low growing shrub at one to four feet mature height.

When it comes to propagating cinquefoil, you have a few choices. One is through purchasing a plant or a division from a neighbor. The best time to plant your cinquefoil plant is in the spring after your local frost-free date or the fall. The best location for this herb is a sunny location in well-draining soil but if that is not possible, cinquefoil can survive in partial shade.

If you have received a division from a friend and it is small, you may want to consider planting the division in a container first. This will give the plant an opportunity to get established before you place it in the ground. But, do not put it in full sun. A location that receives light shade is best until the small division takes hold.

Another choice is through softwood cuttings taken from the new growth in the summer. This should only be done on the shrub varieties. While this will work, you will need to care for the cuttings over winter and plant the next spring.

The third form of propagation is through seed. You can order seed or harvest some from a friend. Planting cinquefoil seeds is simple and can be done directly into the garden after your local frost-free date or started indoors. To begin this process, prepare your chosen garden space by digging a hole six inches wide and deep. Mix one part of each of soil, well seasoned compost, and sand. Fill the hole in and water. Plant a few seeds in this area so that they are ½ inch deep. Lightly cover with soil and mist with water. Repeat this process again making sure that you leave five feet between each hole. This will allow the cinquefoil to spread without confinement.

If you decide you want to plant indoors, plant your seeds in a container or cold frame in the early spring. In 15 to 20 days, your cinquefoil seeds will break ground. Once they are large enough to handle, transplant them into individual containers and care for until established in their pots. After that has happened, move the seedlings to the prepared garden space.

One cautionary tale of this plant is the fact that it does spread through runners that can reach a 5 feet (1.5 meters). This is why it is considered an invasive species.

This herb's use exists in its name. Cinquefoil in Old French means "five leaf."The five leaves was a symbol that represented the five human senses. Knights could have this symbol place on their shields on if they had learned how to control thy self. During medieval times, cinquefoil was used to chase away witches. This may have been why Claire thought she smelled cinquefoil burning along with other herbs during the summoning spell that Geillie preformed with her (Outlander, chapter 24). It was also used in love potions and fishermen would attach this herb to their nets to increase their fish yield.

Since that plant can be found growing wild in pastures, meadows and wasteland, it not surprising that Claire saw it growing in Inverness (Outlander, chapter 1).

When it comes to medical uses, one must make sure that you are talking about European Five Finger Grass *(Potentilla reptans).* The importance of this plant is displayed in its genus name *Potentilla,* which alluded to its "potency." When this plant is applied to open wounds, it is noted that it can reduce skin inflammation and help dry the wound out. It has also been used to treat toothaches, diarrhea, and even fevers.

COLTSFOOT

Tussilago farfara

Part of the scientific name of coltsfoot describes its leaf shape. *Farfarus* is the ancient name for White Popular. While some feel that the leaf does look like White Popular, others think it looks more like a Butterbur. Another interesting fact about this plant is that it did have an older name. *Filius ante patrem* can be translated to mean (son before the father). This describes the growth habit of the coltsfoot. In early spring, golden-colored star-shaped flowers appear. Once the flowers have dwindled down and died, the leaves break ground.

The coltsfoot is just one of fifteen species in the *Tussilago* genus. Those in this genus are known in Latin as the cough dispeller. Teas are made from the coltsfoot to treat coughs. It can also be turned into a poultice and applied to the skin to treat eczema, and sores. An interesting note about coltsfoot is its role in what is referred to as British tobacco. No, there is not tobacco in this product but a basic ingredient is coltsfoot. This perennial herb is mixed with other herbs depending on the ailment, and smoked. The reason that this herb reduces coughing is the fact that it contains mucilage. This sap like substance soothes the throat. Unfortunately, smoking coltsfoots destroys the mucilage, which makes it useless when it comes to treating a cough.

As the name implies, Claire is told that coltsfoot is an herb that can be used to treat coughs by Grannie McNab (Cross Stitch only, chapter 28). Claire also spots coltsfoot growing along the millpond near Lallybroch (Cross Stitch only, chapter 28).

While wildlife loves the seed heads that look like dandelion blowing in the wind for nesting material, there is another unique use for this fluff. Scots Highlanders used to collect the fluff to use as filling for pillows.

Coltsfoot is hardy in USDA Plant Hardiness Zones 4 through 8. If you decide to grow your own, you have a few choices when it comes to propagating. Division is the easiest to do but does require existing plant material. You can also do a root cutting. The least successful is seed. The only way to be successful in seed propagation is to only plant fresh seed. Never store the seed to plant later. The germination rate on the latter is zero.

Where should you plant your coltsfoot? This perennial herb requires full sun but can tolerate some shade. It also requires a damp soil. This is why Claire found this herb growing along a millpond.

While this plant is from Europe, an interesting fact is that it can be found growing wild in North America. As a matter of fact, Breaks Interstate Park in Kentucky utilizes this plant as an attraction along with fractal ferns.

COMFREY

Symphytum officinale

This plant is one of many common names, which includes knitbone, and common comfrey. You may be able to figure out one of the uses for this herb by the common name knitbone. It has been noted that this herb aids in the healing of fractures when applied to the skin. It can also be used to treat swollen veins (phlebitis), which may be why it was noted by Claire to be a possible treatment for hemorrhoids (Cross Stitch only, chapter 1). When Mrs. Fitz suggests that a tea be made from comfrey, she could have been treating an individual with an upset stomach, a heavy menstrual period, cancer, coughing or chest pain (Outlander, chapter 4). Geillis took advantage of the gastric treatment of this herb when she gave it to her husband to stop his farting (Cross Stitch only, chapter 9).

Skin application of comfrey treats wounds and ulcers. Due to modern medicine that Claire was accustomed to, she noted that she would not use comfrey if iodine was existing (Voyager, chapter 40).

Comfrey is a hardy perennial herb in USDA Plant Hardiness Zones 4 through 9. Unlike some plants, comfrey does well in clayey soils. The reason for this is the fact that the root is like a turnip or taproot. This long growing root breaks through a clayey soil with no problem.

This herb requires some room to grow. The mature height of comfrey is around five feet, which can make it look like a shrub.

Environmental requirements of this plant include a sunny to partial shady location that has a well-draining to somewhat soggy soils. Due to the size of this plant, take care not to plant it too close to a smaller plant. It does not take this perennial long to take over an area. Taking this characteristic into account, comfrey is a great herb to plant under fruit trees. The mature size of the comfrey will shade out the weeds while conserving the soil moisture for the orchard.

Methods of propagation for this herb include division, root cuttings, and seed. Division is the easiest to do but requires a plant. Root cuttings are the same. Seed propagation does have its problems. Comfrey seed requires exposure to the cold. Some seed companies do this for you. If you have purchased cold treated seeds then you can expect to get about 80 percent germination rates. To increase this, one may want to place the seeds in a sealable bag with dampened soil. Place the bag in the refrigerator for a couple of weeks prior to planting.

If you want to start your seeds indoors, begin this process in the fall. Prepare a few 4-inch pots as described in the garden primer. Once that is done, fill the pots with soil and add water. Continue to add water until it comes out the bottom of the container. Now, place two seeds per container and mist with water. Place in a sunny location, and monitor the soil moisture. Harden off two weeks prior to your local frost-free date. After that is done, you are ready to plant in the garden.

Planting directly into the garden space begins with preparing the space. In just, remove any unwanted plant material and mix in seasoned manure and/or compost. Comfrey is well known for obtaining all the nitrogen it needs from the soil but the other nutrients have to be added to the soil. This is where the manure and/or compost come into play.

Once the garden space is prepared, sprinkle the seeds on the soil surface, and mist with water. After the seedlings are large enough to handle, thin them so that there is 12 to 16 inches apart. If you want order, consider planting the seedlings in rows that are 36 inches apart.

Since comfrey reseeds itself freely, digging a trench around your plant will help in reducing the number of volunteer plants popping up.

When cold weather moves in, your comfrey will go dormant. This is a great time to add a layer of seasoned manure.

Due to the fact that comfrey soaks up nitrogen from the soil; it is a wonderful ingredient by which to make fertilizer.

CONEFLOWER

Echinacea angustifolia

Echinacea is a genus of flowering plants that contain nine different species, which collectively are referred to as purple coneflower. The Greek term "Echinos" is translated to mean "hedgehog," which describes the large pointed seed head covered in prickly scales. These scales make the seed head look like a hedgehog, hence the name *Echinacea.*

This perennial herb is commonly used to decrease the length of the common cold and flu along with its symptoms. It has also been used to boost the immune system, reduce inflammation, as a febrifuge, antiviral, and antioxidant.

Claire does use *Echinacea* for several of these purposes in the story. First, Claire tries to reduce a fever with purple coneflower while at the Abbey of Ste. Anne de Beaupre (Outlander only, chapter 39). She also takes advantage of the use of this herb as a wound healer. When Jamie is shot by Laoghaire, Claire makes a coneflower ointment to apply to the wound (Voyager, chapter 38).

Purple coneflower thrives in USDA Plant Hardiness Zones 3 through 9. This perennial plant likes a well-draining soil, and a full sun location. If you cannot meet the sun requirement, this plant can tolerate partial shade but the number and size of the blooms will be effected by the amount of shade.

Propagating purple coneflower is done by seed, and root cuttings. Division can occur with purple coneflowers that are three to four years of age in the spring or autumn. While some people have success with this approach, the purple coneflower typical does not like to be disturbed due to its long taproot. If possible, only divide as the clump gets extremely large.

When planning on growing this perennial flower, you will need to plan. First, if you plant your seed outdoors in the fall, then you will not need to perform cold stratification on the seed. Nature will do that for you. Also, *Echinacea* seed takes 15 to 30 days to germinate.

If you plan on starting your purple coneflower seed indoors then you will need to cold stratify your seeds for four to six weeks. To do this, place your seeds in a sealable plastic bag with moistened all-purpose potting soil. Mix the seed and soil together, seal and place in the fridge for the noted time.

In general, after you add the cold treatment time and the local frost-free date, you are looking at planting the seeds indoors in the winter or very early spring.

Planting the seed indoors is easy. Clean and sterilize your container, fill with a well- draining potting soil mix that has been moistened, and sprinkle the seed on the soil surface. Cover with 1/8 inch of soil and mist with water. Place in a sunny location. Continue to monitor the soil moisture. Water when the soil feels dry. In 15 to 30 days, your seeds will germinate. To reduce transplanting shock and damaging the taproot, transplant the seedlings into individual containers as soon as they are large enough to handle. Return to a sunny location. A week prior to your local frost- free date, harden off the plants. After your local frost-free date has passed, plant your seedlings in the prepared garden space.

You may have noticed that I said prepared garden space. Prior to planting your purple coneflower, you will need to do a little garden preparation beyond pulling unwanted plants.

The first step in the garden preparation is to remove the unwanted plant material. Turn the soil over to a depth of 12 to 15 inches. Into this soil, mix in two to four-inches of well seasoned compost. Smooth the surface over. Now you are ready to seed or plant.

When it comes to directly seeding, the process is the same as described previously for indoor propagation. This will need to occur in the fall or very early spring, so that the seeds naturally get the cold treatment.

Since the seed of the purple coneflower is small, it is easier to just sprinkle the seed on the soil surface and sprinkle with 1/8 inch of soil. Mist the soil surface with water to settle the seed and moisten the soil. Avoid watering with a blast of water. This will dislodge the seed and/or bury it too deep where it cannot germinate.

Once your seeds germinate, thin them out so that there is one to three feet between plants, depending on the variety.

If purchase or grow your own purple coneflower plant, you will need to prepare the garden space as described previously. Next, dig a hole that is the same depth as the container and twice the width. Test the hole. Once it is the correct size, very carefully remove the plant from the container. While you always need to tease the roots, this plant is one that you really need to be careful with since it does not like to be transplanted. After you have prepared the roots, place the root ball in the hole and fill in. Water the soil thoroughly. Continue to monitor the soil moisture. Water as need until the root has taken hold.

Due to the fact that the purple coneflower has a taproot, once established it can tolerate some drought.

Upkeep of this plant starts off in the spring. During this time, you will need to add a thin layer of well-seasoned compost. Top the compost with a two inch layer of mulch. This will help control weeds and keep the soil moist. Throughout the season, deadhead the flowers to control volunteer purple coneflowers from popping up everywhere. But, if you want to keep a few seed heads during the winter, go ahead. The seeds of the purple coneflower are the favorite food of many bird species. If your flowers are not standing up, cut the plant down to ground level after the plant is done flowering. As stated before, this plant does not like to be divided, but if you must decrease the clump size then do this only every third spring or fall.

CORYDALIS

Corydalis

The genus *Corydalis* can be a little confusing. One of the common names for this plant is fumitory, which is shared with fumitory *Fumaria officinalis.* While both plants belong to the *Papaveraceae* family, the *Fumaria officinalis* is considered a sub-family of *Papaveraceae.*

It is not made clear as to why Claire digs up this plant while she is at Lallybroch (Outlander, chapter 31), the reason may be based on her botanical knowledge. *Papaveranceae* is under the order of *Ranunculales,* which is informally known as the poppy family. In doing so, Claire may have been harvesting the plant's roots for the treatment of pain. Other aliments this plant's roots has been used to treat include depression, high blood pressure, small intestine spasms, severe nerve damage, and as a mild sedative.

Depending on the species, this perennial plant thrives in USDA Plant Hardiness Zones 3 through 9. The *Corydalis* genus has many species with different requirements. Some like full sun, others like partial shade, and others require full shade. The one requirement that they all have is a soil that remains moisture but is well-draining.

This perennial plant can be propagated through seed, bulb or division. To achieve the greatest level of success, the seed will need to be fresh. It will also need to be cold stratified by placing the seed in a zip up type bag with moistened soil. Place this bag in the fridge for two weeks. Once that time period has passed, remove the seeds. Clean and sterilize a container. Moisten some all-purpose potting soil and fill your container. Sprinkle the treated seeds on top and mist. Depending the light require of the variety, you will place your planted container on a sunny windowsill or in an area that receives indirect sunlight.

Germination will be questionable. It can take one to three months for the seeds to germinate. Once germinated, transplant the seedlings as soon as they are large enough to handle into individual pots.

To give your *Corydalis* seedlings the best chance of survival, keep them in their individual pots for two growing seasons before planting in the garden.

Some individuals have improved their seed germination rate by first exposing the fresh seed to two months of warm temperatures. After that, give them the cold treatment as described previously.

You can also directly seed into the garden space after your local frost-free date. Just keep in mind that this seed does not need to be covered.

While planting seed is one approach that normally is challenging, some species grow from a bulb or rhizome. When it comes to planting the bulb of the *Corydalis* genus, you will need to know what species you are growing. In general, spring flowering species are planted in the fall.

Summer flowering species are planted in the spring. As far as spacing goes, this is dependent on the variety you are planting but it can range from 4 to 16 inches.

Some species of this perennial can be propagated through tubers. In this case, dig a hole by which the tuber fits into comfortably. You want it deep enough to completely cover the tuber but not bury it. The varieties that grow from tubers require three-inch spacing.

The last type of propagation is by way of division. Do not use this approach very often since this plant does not like to have its underground structures disturbed. If you must, divide your plants after they have finished blooming.

While the plants in this genus can easily self seed, they typically do not become invasive. To reduce the number of volunteer plants you have pop up, cut the plant back after it has finished blooming.

COW PARSLEY

Anthriscus sylvestria

Common names abound for this plant. They include cow parsley, wild beaked parsley, wild chervil, keck or mother-die. Another name that it goes by is Queen Anne's lace. While the flower head of both plants look very similar, cow parsley along with Queen Anne's lace belong to the same family (Apiaceae or Umbelliferae). Queen Anne's lace or wild carrot is actually *Daucus carota.*

The scientific name for cow parsley has an interesting story. The story begins with the successor to Aristotle who was a Greek native called Theophrastus. Through his studies of the natural world, he first discovered the process of germination. He also discovered that there was a relationship between plants, climate, and soil. Two of his botanical works that still exist include On the Causes of Plants, and Enquiry into Plants, which were important sources of information during medieval times. In gratitude for his contributions, the genus for cow parsley *(Anthriscus)* was named after him.

The Latin translation for the species name (*sylvestria*) is "of the woods." A looser translation is also used to refer to a plant that grows in the wild.

Due its invasive nature, many states have labeled this plant an invasive species, and banned the sale of seed and/or plants.

Prior to planting in your garden space, check with local extension agent for the plant status.

Cow parsley thrives as a biennial or short-lived perennial in USDA Plant Hardiness Zones 6 through 9. The environmental requirements of this plant are pretty flexible. When it comes to soil, anything will do-but it must be well-draining. Soggy soils will mean the death of this plant. To get the biggest and most beautiful blooms possible, cow parsley needs to be planted in full sun but can tolerate light shade.

When it comes to planting cow parsley seed, you have two choices. You can simply sprinkle on the ground between September and February or May through June. Germination takes 8 to 10 weeks so be patient. Once the seeds germinate, the first year's growth with be vegetative while the second year will produce the beautiful flower head. After the flower is spent, this plant will reseed itself as the parent plant dies. In doing so, you will have a constant supply of cow parsley plants.

In the Outlander book series and STARZ show, the mention of this plant is to simply say that while Frank was visiting Craigh na Dun he tripped and rolled down a hill into a patch of cow parsley (Outlander, chapter 2). Beyond being a natural element in the story, cow parsley has been as a replacement for chervil even though the flavor is stronger. Cow parsley has also been used as a treatment for the common cold, dropsy, stomach problems, and even as a treatment for obesity.

DANDELION

Taraxacum officinale

Yes, dandelion is a common yard weed but it is also a wonderful edible green that is appearing in many grocery stores today. Believe it or not, time has been spent to breed better flavored dandelion greens. The common yard weed dandelion is *Taraxacum officinale subspecies vulgare* but you are not limited to this variety alone. You can also find gourmet types, which includes French dandelion or Vert de Montmagny Dandelion, Amélioré à Coeur Plein Dandelion, Pissenlit Coeur Plein Ameliore Dandelion, Arlington Dandelion, Improved Thick-Leaved Dandelion or Dandelion Ameliore, and Improved Broad Leaved Dandelion. Regardless of what type of dandelion you decide to grow, the key to keeping them less bitter is to grow them in partial shade but in actuality they can grow anywhere in USDA Plant Hardiness Zones 3 through 10.

Dandelions do not have special soil requirement and if you are not concerned with the bitterness of the greens, they can be planted in full sun to partial shade. To the germination rate, you will need to put the small seeds on a dampened paper towel. Place the paper towel in a plastic bag and seal. Put the bag in the refrigerator for one week prior to planting.

While you can get a jump on the season by starting your seeds indoors, I do not recommend this technique. The reason is two-fold. First, I really do not want to take up the space by which to start these seeds early. The second reason is the fact that dandelion seeds are not hard to germinate.

When it comes to planting your seed, prepare the garden space. Next, sprinkle your cold treated seeds on the soil surface after your local frost-free date. There is no reason to cover the seed since dandelion seeds need light to germinate. Mist the soil until it is evenly moist. Keep the soil moist, and in 7 to 14 day you will see evidence of soil germination. Once the seedlings are large enough to handle, thin them out so that there is 8 to 12 inches of space between each plant. At this point, your dandelion plants can take care of themselves.

To keep your dandelions from becoming invasive, never let them go to seed.

Dandelions have been used to treat all sorts of aliments. These include as a laxative, as a treatment for an upset stomach, to increase urine production, skin tonic, blood and digestive tonic. Another uses include treating cancer, and viral infections. While no medical uses are discussed in the book series or STARZ series, it is mentioned that Claire discovers dandelions growing near the millpond by Lallybroch (Cross Stitch only, chapter 28).

DILL

Anethum graveolens

While dill is known for its role in pickling, it also serves another purpose. What is this purpose? Well, it is a great plant that attracts several different types of beneficial insects. This includes honeybees, hoverflies, and Ichneumonid wasps. The smell of dill is also a repellant to the cabbage looper, aphids, squash bugs, and spider mites. This is why planting dill in your vegetable garden is a wonderful idea but avoid planting it near tomatoes and/or carrots.

Dill can be planted in the fall or early spring after your local frost-free date. While you can start your dill indoors, it is not recommend. When this plant is transplanted in the garden space, it typically does not do well.

This annual herb requires a full sun location. When it comes to the soil, it must be well-draining, and moderately rich in organic matter. If this is a problem, add some well seasoned compost and/or manure to the soil. Mix well, and smooth the soil surface over.

Since dill can reach a mature size of two to three feet, it is a good idea to also plant it in a sheltered area. This does not have to be a wall or structure but it can be surrounding plant material in the garden.

The process by which you plant dill is easy. Once the garden space is prepared, simply sprinkle the seed on top. Lightly cover the seed with ¼ inch of soil. Mist the soil with a fine mister to prevent the seed from being pushed down through the soil too deep. Keep the soil evenly moist. Expect to see little green dots begin to appear in 7 to 10 days.

As soon as the seedlings are large enough to handle, space them out at 12 to 18 inches apart.

If you do not have a garden or the garden space, do not delay. Dill can easily be grown in a container. Just keep in mind that it will need to be big enough to hold a two to three foot plant. You will also need to follow the cleaning and sterilizing technique mentioned in the garden primer.

While the "greens" or leaves of the dill are used along with the flower heads, it is a good idea to just leave some of the flowers. This will save you time and effort next year when it comes to planting dill. The seeds in the flower head will drop onto the existing soil. This will allow you to create a permanent dill patch but keep in mind that this herb can quickly become a weed. To prevent dill from becoming a weed, simply pull up any unwanted volunteer dill when it pops up.

In the Outlander book series, and STARZ show, the unique aroma of dill is picked up in Geillie's clothes (Cross Stitch only, chapter 24). This herb is a component of Claire's medical chest, which she uses this herb when fruits and vegetables are scarce during the winter (Dragonfly in Amber, chapter 44). While Claire kept dill in her medicine chest as a source of vitamins, it has also been used to treat digestive problems, urinary tract issues, colds, fevers, menstrual cramps, and even sleep disorders. When applied to the mouth, dill has been used to treat pain and inflammation of not only the mouth but also the throat.

DITTANY

Organum dictamnus or Amaracus dictamnus

This plant is known by several common names, which includes dittany, hop marjoram, and dittany of Crete. This plant has a long history in the medical field, and is noted by Chartemagne and Hippocrates. Chartemagne or Charles the Great mentions this herb in a list of important medieval herbs. Hippocrates suggests using this herb to treat a vast array of aliments.

Dittany of Crete represents love. When given to a loved one, it is viewed as an aphrodisiac. Young men would be encouraged to climb rock cliffs to harvest this herb for their beloved one. These young men were referred to as " Erondades," which comes from another common name for this plant "Eronda." This latter common name is translated to mean "love."

Some believed that goats would seek out this herb after being struck by an arrow, as noted in Aristotle's treatise "The History of Animals," Once the goat found the herb and ate it; the arrow would dislodge and leave the body. This concept was viewed to also work on a man. In Virgil's "Aeneid," it is noted that Venus picks a stalk of dittany of Crete and uses it to treat Aeneas.

In Greek mythology, Zenus give this herb as a gift to Crete. Aphrodite supposedly used this herb. A crown of this herb is often seen on the top of Arternis head. The name dittany is said to come for the Minoan goddess Diktynna. Today, the wild growing dittany of Crete is highly prized, and protected by European law.

In the past, this herb was used to treat digestive issues, easy childbirth, reduce the pain of rheumatism, and even as a snake bite cure. Another use for this herb is in the ritual arena. When burned, it is said to make spirits visible in the smoke and/or stir up passion.

The rocky environment that dittany loves to grow in is noted in the Outlander story. Jamie and Claire first meet Hugh Munro on a hill where dittany of Crete was growing wild (Outlander only, chapter 17).

This perennial herb grows wonderfully in USDA Plant Hardiness Zones 7 through 11. It loves rocky spaces, xeriscaping, and even in containers for indoor or outdoor use. When it comes to the growing requirements of this plant, a well-draining soil that is a little on the dry side is ideal. It also needs to be in full sun.

Dittany of Crete can be propagated through seed, division, and stem cuttings. While it is to assume that dittany of Crete is not growing in your garden, I will start with seed propagation.

You can either directly seed dittany of Crete into the garden space after your local frost-free date or you can start them indoors. If you plan on doing the latter, start the seed between six to eight weeks prior to your frost-free date. Keep in mind that this seed can take up to two weeks to germinate.

To plant the seed, clean and sterilize the chosen container. Fill with a moistened, all-purpose potting soil mix, and sprinkle the seed on top of the soil. Barely cover the seed with soil and mist with water. Place in a sunny location. Monitor the soil moisture but never make it wet. Once the seedlings are large enough to handle either transplant to individual pots or directly into the garden after any chance of frost has passed.

Directly seeding into the garden space follows the same process but should only occur during the very late spring.

Division should happen in March or October. The process is simple, and only requires one to dig up the mother plant. If you want to replant immediately, make sure to cut your divisions large. Small divisions will need to be planted in pots or a cold frame and tended to until they become established. While this herb does thrive in bright sunlight, for this propagation technique it is better to place the small division in an area that is under slight shade. Once the smaller divisions are established, plant in the permanent location.

Taking a cutting is the last propagation technique, and should be performed in June. This particular type of cutting is called basal, and really simply requires one to harvest shoots that are on the side of the plant. What you want to do is to cut these shoots below ground level so that you have some roots attached. Next, clean and sterilize several containers. Allow these to dry, and fill with a well-draining, all purpose potting medium. Plant each one of your basal cuttings in their own pot. Place your planted cuttings in light shade, and monitor soil moisture. Once the cutting has rooted into the soil, plant in the garden. How do you know if the herb has rooted? Gently tug on the cutting. If you feel resistance then it has rooted.

To aid in developing a strong root system, pinch off any flower buds.

This small statured upright subshrub whose mature height is 5 to 6 inches and has a spread of 16 inches, look wonderful in a hanging basket inside or out. If you decide to grow dittany of Crete indoors, make sure that it gets enough sunlight. To mimic the outdoor environment, water sparingly during the winter but never let the soil dry out.

DOCK

Rumex

As you may have noted, only the genus of dock is listed. The reason for this is there are several different kinds of dock. This includes broadleaf dock *(Rumex obtusifolius),* yellow dock (*Rumex crispus)* and French sorrel *(Rumex scutatus),* just to name a few but this genus includes over 200 species. This perennial weed can be found growing in on disturbed land in USDA Plant Hardiness Zones 5 through 9.

In the Outlander book series and STARZ show, dock is simply mentioned as a wrap for the trout that Jamie caught (Cross Stitch only, chapter 16). In the culinary world, the large leaves of the dock can be used to wrap meat or vegetables and stem it over a fire. Beyond being an edible, dock root can be steeped into a bitter tea, which can be used as a laxative or a detoxing agent for the liver.

It is suggested that if you simply want to use dock for culinary purposes then you should grow French sorrel *(Rumex scutatus).* Regardless as to why you want to grow dock, the first step is plant the seed. This seed can be planted directly into the garden or started indoors. Keep in mind though that it will take up to two weeks for the seeds to germinate.

Before we get to planting dock seed there is one word of caution. Dock is considered a broadleaf weed due to its invasive nature. It not only spreads by seed but also through rhizomes. To reduce the chances that dock will take over, consider planting your seed in a container. But if using this approach, make sure to clean and sterilize the container prior to planting. When it comes to the planting medium for dock, combine equal parts of an all-purpose potting soil and well seasoned compost and/or manure.

Regardless of where you plant your dock seed, the process is simple. It only requires one to sprinkle the seed on the soil surface after your local frost-free date has passed. Once that is done, cover with ¼ inch of soil, and mist to moisten. Keep the soil evenly moist. In 7 to 14 days, you will see your dock seedlings appear. As soon as the dock seedlings are large enough to handle, space the seedlings so that there is 12 inches between plants.

The best environment for dock is in a soil that is moist and rich. The sun requirement is that of full sun, but it can thrive in partial shade.

As with any green, the key to extending the season is to pick the leaves often.

To keep dock under control, remove the flower stalk as soon as it appears. This will prevent seed production.

If you have an ample supply of dock but want it somewhere else, the best approach is to divide the plant. This should be done in the early spring and/or autumn. The key to this technique is to dig deep to harvest the rhizome. Once you have the rhizome, you can just plant it in its new location. This dock will leaf out the following spring.

ELECAMPANE

Inula helenium

Elecampane has two common names that describe old-time uses of this perennial herb. Horseheal is the first common name. Those involved in veterinary practices would use this herb to treat pulmonary problems of horses. When this herb was applied to the sores on sheep, it caused a scab-hence scabwort.

In the Outlander book series, and STARZ show, elecampane is noted twice. The first use comes from burning it. Claire puts some elecampane in the charcoal brazier to sweeten the smoke (Outlander, chapter 40). The concept of sweetening the smoke may not be the aroma but human relations. Elecampane is sometimes added to love charms because it is believed that this herb attracts beneficial spirits and/or positive interaction between humans.

The other mentioning of this herb comes from when Claire finds a jar of elecampane at Mr. Heugh's apothecary. She tells Mr. Heugh that this herb can be used to treat sticky-sounding coughs (Voyager, chapter 43).

Elecampane has been used to treat all sorts of coughs. This herb makes bringing up and expelling phylum easier. In doing so, it has been used to treat such aliments as whooping cough, asthma, and bronchitis. It has also been used to treat the cough associated with tuberculosis.

A unique use for this herb is in the treatment of intestinal worms, which can cause nausea and diarrhea. It has been found that elecampane contains a chemical that kills several different types of intestinal worms.

The importance of this herb as a treatment for stomach issues can even be found in the Bible. Elecampane root was added to wine to make a digestive wine, which was called potio Paulina or "drink of Paul." This drink is referred to in the Bible by St. Paul. He states that one should consume a little wine daily for stomach health or "use a little wine for thy stomach sake."

Elecampane is not difficult to grow. It is a hardy perennial in USDA Plant Hardiness Zones 2a through 8a. It needs a full sun environment with well-draining soil that remains damp but it can tolerate partial shade. When it comes to sun or soil moisture, the level of moisture in the soil is the most important. If the soil is too wet, the plant will rot. On the other hand, soil that is too dry will cause the plant to die.

When it comes to propagating this herb, you can either grow it from seed or root cuttings. This herb is no longer widely grown so finding a source of root cuttings may be a challenge around your gardening friends. Seeds are available, but both techniques will be covered.

Seeds can be started indoors but can take two weeks to two months to germinate. You may not want to care for your seeds that long. On the other hand, you can directly seed your elecampane into the garden space, cold frame in the spring or beginning of autumn. When planting your seed in the spring, plant a week or two prior to your local frost-free date and cover the seed with a thin layer of soil. Water the garden space after it has been planted. Keep the soil evenly moist. Once the seeds germinate, and they are large enough to handle, thin so that there is 12 to 18 inches between each plant.

The second form of propagation is through root cuttings, which can be taken either in the spring or autumn. To take a root cutting in the spring, dig up the mother plant, and cut off a two inch piece that has an eye or bud on it. You should then immediately replant into the garden in rows that are three feet apart, and plants that are 12 to 18 inches apart. When it comes to the depth of the root cutting, just make sure the root is covered.

When you take root cuttings in the autumn, the process is the same as above, except you do not directly replant. What you will need to do is to fill a flat or large pot with a soil mixture of equal parts potting soil and sand. Another choice is to use a cold frame. Regardless of what you choose; plant your root cuttings in this soil mixture as described previously. Once the root cuttings are planted, place in a room such as a garage that stays between 50 and 60 degrees Fahrenheit. Keep them in this location throughout the autumn and winter. Once your local frost-free date has passed, remove your root cuttings. Plant those that have eyes or buds that are ready to leaf out in the prepared garden space.

EYEBRIGHT

Euphrasia officinalis

As you have guessed, eyebright has been used to treat eye problems for centuries. This included pink eye and any inflammation of the eyelid. When this herb was taken orally, this herb treated such issues as hay fever, colds, and even sore throats. In the past, this herb was part of British Herb Tobacco. This substance was smoked and inhaled. The inhaling of the burning herbal tobacco reduced the inflammation of the lungs and eased the effects of respiratory problems.

When it comes to growing eyebright, one must first understand this plant. Eyebright is an annual that thrives in

USDA Plant Hardiness Zones 1 through 9. The unique of this plant though comes from the fact that it is a semi-parasite that feeds on the roots of grasses. The eyebright seeks out grass roots and when they come in contact with those roots, they produce a nodule. From this nodule, they harvest nutrition from the grass plant. This harvesting of nutrition is minor and does not harm the grass plant.

Since this plant is an annual, when the area receives a killing frost the plant and its roots die.

While this plant is a semi-parasitic and you may not want it growing around your grass, it does produce bright green foliage and tiny blooms that are white or light purple with some yellow highlights. The mature height of this plant is two to eight inches, which makes it a great match for a grassland or field because it will not shade the grass.

When it comes to propagating eyebright, the only approach is through seed. This plant does not transplant well and in doing so, you will need to directly seed into a sunny location. But, without cold treatment, do not expect the seeds to germinate.

If you live in an area that receives cold temperatures during the fall and winter, you can directly seed into the prepared grassland. On the other hand, if your winters are not three months long, you will need to create that environment by placing your seeds in a sealable plastic bag along with moistened soil. Put the bag in the refrigerator and only remove after the seeds have been in the fridge for three months.

Prior to planting, you will need to prepare the grassland. While grass needs to be present, the eyebright also needs room to grow. To create this space, pull up 40 to 50 percent of the grass. Next, loosen up the soil to a depth of one inch and broadcast the seed over the area. Since the seeds are small, only mist the area and keep it evenly moist.

Except watering, leave this annual alone and it will award you with blooms from July through September.

Eyebright is mentioned as a plant that was seen on top of the hill where Jamie and Claire first meet Hugh Munroe (Outlander, 17).

FENNEL

Foeniculum vulgare

In the Outlander book series, and STARZ show, fennel is mentioned twice but it is not clear as to whether the herb or the vegetable is being described. Fennel is noted to be growing in the herb garden at Castle Leoch (Cross Stitch only, chapter 6). When Duncan's phantom limb is causing him pain, Claire wonders if she can give him some relief by combining fennel and horehound (Voyager, chapter 43). While there was no direct connection between consuming fennel seed and/or bulb-and pain relief, this herb/vegetable does contain choline. This nutrient helps reduce inflammation and aids in the transmission of nerve impulses. Other uses for fennel are for digestive problems, such as gas and heartburn. Upper respiratory problems have also been treated with fennel.

Believe it or not, the herb/vegetable also contains estrogen. In doing so, some women have used fennel to increase sex drive, increase milk production and ease the pain from child birthing.

When the fennel is turned into a powder and a poultice is made, some believe that the application of this poultice is a treatment for snakebite.

Whether you are growing the herb fennel or vegetable, both are typically grown as annuals. But the herb fennel is a perennial in USDA Plant Hardiness Zones 8a to 10b while the vegetable fennel is a biennial.

To begin the planting conversation on fennel, we will start with *Foeniculum vulgare* or herb fennel. The plant requires full sun in well-draining and fertile soil. To improve the fertility of the soil, incorporate a good amount of well-seasoned compost and/or manure.

Herb fennel does not transplant well. You will need to directly seed into the prepared garden space in the autumn, or spring after your local frost-free date. To give herb fennel the space it needs, plant your seeds every 12 inches. If planting in rows, space them out so that there is three feet between them. As you plant your seed, cover with ¼ inch of soil. Once all the seeds have been planted, water the soil until it is evenly moist. Monitor soil moisture. Never let the soil dry out, and in 12 to 18 days you will see your herb fennel seedlings appear.

If you do not have the garden space by which to plant herb fennel, do not give up. This herb can also be planted in a large container. When selecting your container, make sure it is big enough to hold a plant with a mature size of three to four feet.

When it comes to care, herb fennel takes care of itself. You may need to stake the fronds up off the ground to reduce plant diseases. Also, if you live in the hardiness zones listed previously, you may want to mulch your herb fennel with four-inches of mulch. This can be ground up leaves, straw, or evergreen boughs.

Please note that herb fennel can be propagated through root cuttings and crown divisions but this will not be covered.

The vegetable fennel is called *Foeniculum vulgare* var. *azoricum* or Florence fennel. It is planted the same as the herb variety. While you can use the leaves for flavoring of the herb type, it is not recommended to harvest the leaves of the growing vegetable type. Cutting the leaves has the potential to decrease the bulb size.

To get the most out of your fennel, do not plant near other herbs or vegetables. It has a tendency to cross pollinate with herbs such as dill. This cross pollinate will affect the taste of the parts of the fennel.

FOXGLOVE

Digitalis purpurea

Foxglove, collectively, has over twenty species. Some are easily obtainable at your local garden nursery and/or seed catalogue. Others are only locally available, and some are so abnormal that plant collector swoop to pick them up for their collection. The *Digitalis* genus is considered to be a biennial or short-lived perennial. Some people believe that foxglove is a perennial. The reason for this is the fact that this plant easily reseeds itself so you never really miss the plants dying after their second season.

When one thinks about foxglove, they also associate it with the term digitalis, which is also connected with a drug that is used in the treatment of congestive heart failure. While this is true, only one species of foxglove is actually used to make digoxin (Lanoxin). *Digitalis lanata* or wooly/Grecian foxglove is the plant by which this drug is obtained. Before you leap out to buy this plant, keep in mind that in some areas in North America, this plant is classified as a noxious weed.

Due to immigration, and interest in botany, the foxglove genus can be found all over the world. In the past though, this plant was limited to western and Eastern Europe, which is where Claire found it growing in the herb garden at Castle Leoch (Outlander, chapter 6). Claire thinks she smells foxglove burning when she does the summoning spell with Geillie (Outlander, chapter 24). While nothing could be found on this topic, the offensive odor of the fresh leaves may be what Claire smelled.

When Alex Randall was coughing and having heart palpitations, Claire made a digitalin extract from the dried leaves of the foxglove (Dragonfly in Amber, chapter 39).

Beyond using foxglove to treat heart issues, it has also been used to treat constipation, epilepsy, asthma, headache, and to encourage vomiting. When applied to the skin, foxglove is used to help wounds and/or burns heal.

In North America, *Digitalis* thrives in USDA Plant Hardiness Zones 3 through 8. When it comes to growing requirements, this plant needs a rich, well-draining soil that is in partial shade. The key to the light requirement is "partial." Whether your foxglove is receiving too much light or shade, the blooms will be affected. The only exception is if you live in the northern parts of North America. In this environment, foxgloves can be grown in full sun.

Foxglove propagation is either through seed or division. While you can start your seed indoors, I do not recommend it. Foxglove typically does not like to be transplanted, which can cause the plant not to bloom its second year.

If you want to plant your seed indoors anyway, the process is simple. Clean and sterilize a four-inch pot. Fill with an all-purpose potting soil that has been moistened. Sprinkle the seed on top of the soil surface. Do not cover with soil. Mist the soil until you see moisture coming out the bottom of the container. Place clear plastic or a piece of glass on top of the planted pot. Put your container indoor location that is shady. Be diligent with the soil moisture. Check often and water as needed. Germination of foxglove seed can take up to 21 days.

Once the seeds have germinated, remove the clear plastic or glass. As soon as the seedlings are large enough to handle, thin them out so that there is six to eight inches between each plant.

Continue to care for your foxglove seedlings until your local frost-free date has passed. Once that has happened, plant your foxglove seedlings in the garden. When it comes to the spacing though, it is strictly dependent on the variety you are growing but a good rule of thumb is to allow 18 inches between plants.

Care of the foxglove is simple. First, monitor the soil moisture. Never let it dry out completely. Second, to control the number of foxglove plants you have, deadhead the flower stalk as soon as the flowers are finished. Doing this garden chore will do two things. One, it will help control the numbers as stated before, and two; it can encourage the plant to bloom again. If you do see volunteer foxglove seedlings appearing in your garden space, simply dig them up when they are small and transplant them in a new location or just compost.

To protect your foxglove plants and keep them healthy, cut them back to ground level in the fall. Top the plants with three to five-inch mulch layer of leaves and/or straw. This mulch layer will protect the plants from the cold wind, conserve soil moisture, and help control weeds.

After your local frost-free date, gently move away the mulch from the foxglove plants to resume the growing season.

While foxglove plants do take room to grow, there is an alternative, and that is container gardening. Yes, I know foxglove typically does not like to be transplanted, but if done carefully it can be successfully accomplished.

Due to the fact that the foxglove can have a mature height of one to eight feet and a width of one to three feet, it makes a create "thriller" in the container garden formula. When making your container garden, you need to first put on a pair of gloves. Some foxgloves have little hairs, which can irritate the skin, and the plant is poisonous. When working with this plant, it is just a good idea to wear hand protection.

The first step in the container garden process is to find a very large pot that has drainage holes. Once you have found the proper container, clean and sterilize it. Let it dry completely. Put some drainage material in the bottom. Fill with a fifty-fifty mixture of all-purpose potting soil and well- seasoned compost. Now you are ready to plant your foxglove.

Since this plant will be your "thriller," it is best to center the plant; but before you do, let me explain something. Most of the foxglove plants that you buy are second- year plants. What this means is that they will bloom the year you plant them in your container. You will not need to hold them over to enjoy blooms the next year.

Now that you have your foxglove plant, gently remove it from its container. Very lightly tease the roots but try really hard not to do it too much. You want to loosen the soil up enough so that the roots know to grow outwards. Next, dig a hole in the center of your container that is deep enough to hold the plant so that its soil level is equal to that of the container.

After planting the foxglove, you will need plants that are "fillers" and "spillers." The key to this is to make sure that these plants have the same growing requirements as the foxglove.

Once your container garden is planted, add water until you see it come out the bottom of the container. Check the soil moisture often. This is very important since container gardens dry out fast.

Now that you know how to grow foxglove, you may be wondering where the name originated. A hint can be found in some of the common names, which include fairy's glove, witch's bell, and folk's glove. As one may guess, the common name is describing the bloom. The name for this plant is an old one. It comes from a story that talks about the foxglove growing in the woods where the "good" fairies lived. It is said that the "bad" fairies collected the blooms. When these "bad" fairies would come upon a fox, they would give them these blooms to put on toes so that they could walk quietly while hunting.

FUMITORY

Fumaria officinalis

Fumitory is known by several common names, which includes earth smoke, fumus vapor, fumewort, and fumus terra just to name a few. While this plant was originally from Europe, it has easily naturalized itself across North America. You may have noticed a theme when it comes to the common name of this plant. The description of smoke or vapor comes from the shape and color of the leaves along with the smell of the roots. From a distance, the small, gray-green leaves resemble smoke. On the other hand, when the roots were dug up, the aroma reminds one of smoke. It is not clear which description of smoke the Latin term "fumus" was describing, but never-the- less, this characteristic became part of the name.

While there are several different types of fumitory—which is limited to the geographic area you live in—only the annual variety will be covered. Regardless of which variety you choose, keep in mind that insects do not visit the blooms. In doing so, this plant has developed that ability to self-fertilize and is so successful at this that all seeds set. This fact is why this plant easily becomes invasive.

Since we will only be covering the annual variety, the first step to propagating this plant is site selection. This plant needs a lot of room, so plan accordingly. What I mean by a lot of room is the fact that the plants need to be spaced 10 inches apart in a location that receives full sun to partial shade. It really is not picky about soil type, but it does need to be well-draining, and nutrient rich. To aid in the latter requirement, you may want to add some compost to the garden space when you prepare it for planting.

After the preparation of the garden space has occurred--and you are ready to plant in March or April—mark off space in 10 inch increments. At each one of the marked spots, plant your fumitory seed 2 inches deep. Once all the planting is completed, water the garden space.

Keep the space evenly moist. In 20 to 30 days, you should see evidence that your seeds have germinated. At this point, continue to water when needed, but as the season progresses back off on the watering.

To reduce the chances that fumitory is going to be invasive in your garden, make sure to remove the spent flowers as soon as they fade away. Another technique is to leave the soil alone. It has been found that fumitory seed's germination rate is reduced if the soil is left undisturbed. This was particularly true when it came to agricultural fields.

In the story, fumitory was a plant that made up part of the herb garden in Castle Leoch (Cross Stitch only, chapter 6). While it is not noted as a plant remedy in the story, it has been used to treat intestinal problems such as irritable bowel syndrome, and constipation. Fumitory has also treated skin conditions, heart problems, and even eye irritations.

Two remaining uses for this plant include a dye, and as a means of getting rid of evil spirits. When it comes to a dye, the flowers were harvested and used to make yellow-colored wool.

The expelling of evil spirits would occur when the plant was burned. Ancient people also believed that the propagation of fumitory did not come from seed but from vapors that would come from the earth itself.

GENTIAN

Gentiana

Gentaina is a genus that contains over 200 species. Out of the 200, only a handful is cultivated for gardens. While most of those grown, bloom either in the early spring or fall, there still are a few that produce colorful blooms in mid-summer. Regardless of the growing period, gentians are considered hardy perennials in USDA Plant Hardiness Zones 3 through 9.

All gentians require a soil to have a good amount of organic material. The soil needs to be evenly moist. The light requirement is a little trickier. If you live in an area that has cool summers then a location that receives full sun is the best choice. On the other hand, if you live in a warm climate where the sun is intense then you will need to plant gentian in a location by which it is shaded from the midday sun.

Out of all the limiting factors, the soil ph is critical. Why is this? Well, some species of the gentian require acidic soil while others need a soil that is more alkaline. This picture is confused more when you take into account those plants that do not care. In doing so, make sure that you are familiar with the growing requirements of the gentian species you choose.

As a warning to plant collectors, do not harvest from the wild. They do not survive transplanting in this way. The best approach is to find a nursery that carries the plants and/or rock or alpine garden society that is willing to share knowledge and some gentians.

Propagation of gentians occurs in two ways, which includes seed, and cuttings. Both of these require plants. If you decide to go the seed route, you will need to plant the seed in a cold frame as soon as it is ripe. Delaying planting time decreases drastically the germination rate. Once you have harvested your seed, plant in an open cold frame in the spring. But, the success you will have with this approach is limited. The age of the seed and its viability is one limiting factor. The second is the fact that the roots of the seedlings are easily damaged. The best success comes from utilizing cuttings.

The first step of this process is mixing-up the planting medium. This special formula is equal parts of loam, horticulture sand, and grit. Once that is done, clean and sterilize your chosen container. Next, add water to the DIY planting medium, and mix until evenly moist. Fill the container will soil.

At this point, wipe down your knife with rubbing alcohol. Take a four-inch cut at an angle. Remove all the leaves except the top rosette. Using a pencil, make a hole in the planting medium, and place your cutting in the hole up to the rosette. To keep the rosette dry, top with pea gravel or smaller grit.

Keep the cuttings medium evenly moist and place them in an area that receives filtered sunlight. In four to six weeks, you should have a sign of root development. The best test for this without removing the plant material is by gently tugging on the cutting. If you feel resistance then chances are your cutting has rooted.

To reduce transplanting stress, harvest the cutting(s) so that there is as much planting medium around the roots as possible. If done right, your transplanted cutting(s) will never know they have been removed.

In the Outlander series, Claire uses gentian ointment on Charles Stuart's hand, which had been bitten by Louise de Rohan's monkey (Dragonfly in Amber, chapter 11).

Gentians have a long history as a plant used for medical purposes. Gentius, the King of Illyria (180-167 B.C.), has the distinction of discovering the medical value of this plant, which the genus was named. This was noted by both Pliny and Dioscorides. In the Middle Ages, this genus was used to treat cases of poisoning. In 1552, Tragus was the first to mention using gentians as a treatment for wounds.

Beyond using this plant for wound treatment, it also is noted to treat numerous digestive problems, muscle spasms, and cancer. The germ-killing affects of this genus may be why it has been used to treat wounds, and as a parasitic worm killer.

GERMANDER

Teucrium

The germander belongs to the genus *Teucrium.* This genus is known to have fragrant foliage and a flower spike-covered in white, blue, pink, yellow, pale green or lavender blooms. Germander thrives in USDA Plant Hardiness Zones 5 through 11 where the soil is a little on the dry side, and the sun is shining bright. While it does its best in sunny locations, it can take partial shade.

One of the unique aspects of this plant is the fact that bees of all kinds love them. Another characteristic of this evergreen perennial is its ability to tolerate pruning. This is why it makes a beautiful hedge, topiary or outline plant for a knot garden.

Propagation can occur through seed, division, and cuttings, which the latter two should occur in the spring.

Seed propagation can occur outdoors in the late spring prior to the last late frost and/or autumn. When using this technique, only sprinkle the seed on the prepared soil surface. If you decide that you want to start your seed indoors, then you will need to count back eight weeks prior to your local frost-free date. Once you have that date, plan accordingly by preparing your container(s).

Next, fill with a dampened all-purpose potting soil. Sprinkle the seed on top, mist with water, and place on a sunny window sill. This latter approach will take a month before the seeds germinate. During this time, do not forget to monitor soil moisture so that it remains a little on the dry side.

A week prior to your local frost-free date, harden off the seedlings by gradually exposing them to their new garden environment.

Once the hardening off process is finished, transplant the seedlings in the garden space at 8 to 16 inches apart. The distance is determined by the use.

Left unintended, this short shrub will grow wild and spindly. To encourage bushy growth, prune back the shrub fifty percent after blooming. Fertilize yearly with a balanced fertilizer.

When it comes to the other forms of propagation, make sure to perform these tasks in the spring. Division of this plant is simple. It only requires one to dig up the parent plant, split the root mass, and plant it back into a hole that is the same depth but twice the width.

Cutting can be taken from the pruning you do, or new cuttings taken later in the spring. To begin this process, starts off with cleaning and sterilizing the container(s). Fill with dampened potting mix. Wipe down the knife you will be using to take the cuttings with rubbing alcohol. Now, you are ready to take the cuttings, which should be at an angle. Once you have cuttings, use a pencil to make a hole in the dampened soil. Push the soil back around the cutting. Repeat as needed. Place in a sunny location and monitor soil moisture. In four to six weeks, check for rooting by gently pulling on the cutting. If it resists, the cutting has rooted, and ready to plant in the garden. If no resistance is felt, continue to care for the cuttings for another four weeks, and check again.

The Outlander storyline notes that at Helwater was growing on the grounds (Voyager, chapter 14). The only noted one that has any noted medical use is the water germander (*Teucrium scordium*). This plant in the past has been used as an antidote for poison, and an antiseptic. Some individuals also use it as a treatment for fevers, hemorrhoids, and even intestinal parasitic worms.

GINGER

Zingiber officianle

Ginger has a long history when it comes to the medical uses of this herb. One of the most common uses for this plant comes from its ability to treat an assortment of "stomach problems." This includes morning sickness, colic, and nausea caused by cancer and HIV/AIDS treatments, along with surgery-induced upset stomach. To take advantage of ginger's ability to settle the stomach, Claire prepares a tea of grated ginger to treat Jamie's motion and/or seasickness while they are on the Artemis (Voyager, chapter 41). Due to ginger's fibrous nature, this herb is also used as a laxative.

Beyond medical uses, this herb is a valued in the culinary world. Since we "eat" with all our senses, ginger is used in soups as a fragrance, and as a flavoring. To make the food more desirable while on the Artemis, Claire bribed Mr. Murphy, the cook, with ginger and other spices (Voyager, chapter 41).

When it comes to growing this herbaceous perennial, you will first need to note what USDA Plant Hardiness Zone is yours. Ginger is hardy in zones 9 through 12 only. If you do not live in these zones, do not fret. You can still grow your own ginger but you have to winter it indoors.

Believe it or not, ginger is one of a long list of herbs that you can get your plant material from the produce section of your local grocery store. The key to using herbs from the produce section is to select the freshest items possible. This means that your ginger root should be plump with a few knots or nibs on the root. Once you have your ginger root selected, soak it in a cup full of slightly warm water overnight. The next morning, remove your ginger root and cut into two inch segments. At this point, you can do three things. One, you can poke toothpicks into the two inch piece of root and suspend it over a glass of water so that one-third of it is in the water. Keep it in the glass until roots are about one inch long. At that point, your ginger is ready to plant.

Another technique is to simply plant your soaked ginger root in a container. To do this requires one to clean and sterilize a container that has drainage holes. This requirement is very important since ginger root can easily rot. Once the container is prepared, and the drainage material has been added to the bottom of the pot, fill the container with equal parts of an all-purpose potting soil medium, mixed with seasoned compost or worm manure, peat moss, and perlite. This DIY planting medium keeps the soil loose and well-draining while moist at the same time. At this point, plant your ginger root two inches down, and water.

Place your potted ginger root, on a window sill that receives filtered light until you can take the pot outside. To keep the required humidity level up, put your planted ginger root on a humidity tray, and mist daily.

The last technique is to directly plant your ginger outside. Keep in mind that this only works in USDA Plant Hardiness Zones 9 through 11. The key to growing ginger outside beyond the hardiness zones is location. Ginger requires a location that is at least partially shady but if you can, make sure to place it in a fully shady area that is protected. Also, the soil needs to be moist, well-draining and fertile. If you do not have the perfect soil conditions, add a good amount of well-seasoned compost before planting your ginger.

If you are growing ginger for your own use, only dig up the rhizome(s) when the plant has gone dormant. This dormancy is noted in the fall/winter with the foliage has died back.

GOLDENROD

Solidago

Goldenrod belongs to a genus (*Solidago),* which includes environmentally-limiting species. As an example, the *Solidago sempervirens L.* or seaside goldenrod is limited to beaches and coasts. The adaptability of these plants categorizes it as a native in the United States.

The genus name of goldenrod comes from the Latin term "solidare," which translated means "to make whole." While this translation does not provide a hint as to the use, in (Dragonfly in Amber, chapter 20) this plant was one of the herbs used by Claire to treat Mary Hawkins wounds. Yes, goldenrod has been used to aid in the healing of wounds, but it can also be used to reduce pain and inflammation of many different body parts. Using goldenrod to increase urine production to flush the system is another use. Treatment for diseases such as diabetes and infections caused by tuberculosis have been created using goldenrod.

A little unknown use for a particular species of goldenrod is that of synthetic rubber. Thomas Edison, along with Henry Ford, noticed that the *Solidago sempervirens* or seaside goldenrod, produce a thick, sticky sap. Through planting breeding, Thomas Edison was able to create a 12 foot tall plant that produced 12 percent rubber. He then used this rubber to make tires for the Model T that Henry Ford had given him.

Another interesting fact is that there is one species of goldenrod, shorts goldenrod, that is federally protected. Shorts goldenrod is so rare that it was put on the Federal Endangered Species list in 1985. Originally, this plant was found only growing along bison trails, but others groups of these plants have also been found growing out of fissures of limestone. While other species of goldenrod seed seems to be spread by the wind, the shorts goldenrod seems to have a relationship with the bison. For this reason, propagating shorts goldenrod has not been successful to date.

In many areas of the country, goldenrod is considered a weed, but its soil-holding ability and food source for insects, makes it invaluable. If you have a friend with a nice patch of goldenrod, simply ask if you can dig some up. This can be done either in the spring or fall. The reason that this is possible is because goldenrod spreads by rhizomes—or woody caudices--which also makes this perennial hard to control.

Dividing goldenrod is easy. The first step is to prepare the proper garden space. Goldenrod likes a soil that is fertile and heavy in nature. It also needs to be able to hold moisture. A soil type for the majority of goldenrod species would be one high in clay. The exception would be the seaside goldenrod.

Once you have your location selected, prepare the garden space by removing any unwanted plant material. Next, dig up your donor golden by digging up the entire plant. Using a sterilized knife, cut through the rhizomes to divide the mother plant into several sections. Replant the divided mother plant. When it comes to your division(s), make sure that the hole is the same depth while the width is twice the diameter of the root ball.

Place division in the hole, fill in, and water. Monitor soil moisture until the divided goldenrod has taken root.

If you have no local garden sources, you can purchase seed but do not harvest from the wild. The seed is easy to start. This process starts off in the spring in a cold frame that has been filled with well- seasoned compost. Simply sprinkle the seed on the soil surface and barely cover with soil. Mist the compost. In a few weeks, you will begin to see little dots of growth in the cold frame. Continue to add water to the cold frame as needed. Once the goldenrod seedlings are large enough to handle, transplant into prepared, individual containers, and care for throughout the growing season until next spring. At this time, the goldenrod seedlings can be planted in the proper garden space.

GOLDENSEAL

Hydrastis canadensis L.

Goldenseal is one of those unique plants that have an interesting story. First, the term goldenseal is the European common name for this North American native. The Native People of North American called this plant yellow root. The reason for this was the fact that the root was yellow. Native People used yellow root to dye their clothing yellow. They also used it in a limited way to treat health aliments such as cancer. When the Europeans landed on the shores of North America, they noticed Native People harvesting this plant's roots. When these roots are cut open, a yellow circle is produced, hence the term "goldenseal." This term described prior knowledge that Europeans had of wax seals that were used to seal letters. This plant was so valued that it was taken back to Europe around 1760. Today, goldenseal/yellow root is one of the few plants that are listed on the endangered species list on two continents. While you can still buy goldenseal root, the wild plants are the ones endangered. To protect the wild plants, it is now against the law to sell goldenseal/yellow root across country boundaries--along with strict documentation as to where the plant material was harvested.

The medical value of this plant was reinforced in 1905 by the U.S. Department of Agriculture. This agency noted that goldenseal/yellow root had market value for farmers and could be grown as an alternative crop for cultivation in USDA Plant Hardiness Zones 5 through 8.

When it comes to growing goldenseal/yellow root, you have three choices. This includes seed, rhizome, and/or rootlets. Goldenseal seed is normally not sold but if you have a friend, you may be able to get some seed to start your own. Keep in mind though that planting goldenseal seed is not as simple as it may seem and many times it is unreliable.

The first step in this process is to prepare the seed. What this means is you will need to harvest the "ripe fruit" from the goldenseal plant. This fruit is easy to find since it looks like a red raspberry.

Next, crush the fruit to release the seed from the pulp. At this point, place the pulp and seed in a bowl of water and let it sit for a couple of days to ferment. While you are waiting for this to happen, you can prepare the garden space. This space must be shady, or create shade with a lean-to frame covered with shade cloth. The soil also needs to be well-draining.

While you can plant your seed in their permanent location, a better approach is to plant the seed in a raised bed or cold frame. Planting the seed in this way allows one to control the shade and moisture level.

Regardless of where you plant your seed, the next step is to rinse off the seed after the fruit flesh has been cleaned off. Next, plant the seed one-quarter to half an inch deep every inch. Cover the seeds with several inches of leaf mulch. Water the seeds. Continue to monitor soil moisture. Never let the seeds dry out. Do not be discouraged about the germination rate of goldenseal seed. It is not uncommon for germination to take two growing seasons. Also, do not transplant the seedlings until they are two years old, and have formed a rhizome.

The most common propagation method for goldenseal is through rhizome cuttings. When it comes to processing the rhizomes for plant propagation begins with cleaning your pruners with rubbing alcohol. Next, take a ruler and start a cut at the half-inch mark or larger. The key is to make sure that there is at least one bud on the rhizome and fibrous roots attached. On the same line as the rhizome, root cutting can be taken. This technique is normally not very successful and only the roots farthest from the rhizome should be cut as described above for the rhizome.

Next, plant the prepared rhizome in a garden bed by which weeds have been removed. A weedy bed is death to goldenseal plants, so make your planting time worth your time with preparation. Once the bed is prepared, lay down the prepared rhizomes in rows that are 6 to 12 inches apart. Space the individual rhizomes six inches apart, with the bud facing up, and the rhizome itself just covered with soil.

Cover the area with a thick layer of hardwood leaves or shredded hardwood mulch. In the early spring, rake back the mulch to the point that there is only one to inches left on the soil surface. This will make it easier for the goldenseal to emerge through the ground.

While there has been a lot of research on what is the best environment for planting goldenseal in the wild, some of the results can be at a depth that you just throw your hands up and say forget it. To prevent you from doing this, I have taken the research and broke it down to the basics.

First, planting goldenseal on a slight slope is essential. The slope allows the soil to remain moist--but not wet. Another factor of the soil is that it needs to be rich in organic matter, and have a pH of 5.5 to 6.5. Second, the amount of shade that is needed is around 70 to 75 percent. Third, believe it or not, nature will give you clues as to where goldenseal should be planted. A tall hardwood forest comprising of maple, basswood, hickory, tulip popular, and white oak is ideal. Understory plants to look for include mayapple, ginseng, trillium, bloodroot, and black cohosh.

One of the most fabled uses for goldenseal is as a drug concealer. There is no evidence that taking goldenseal masks drug use in the urine. Due to a certain chemical found in this herb, goldenseal is used to treat infections, such as urinary, common colds, pink eye, and as a mouthwash for sore gums. It has also been used as an antitumor or cytotoxic treatment. Women sometimes use this herb as a treatment for menstrual pain and swelling.

Claire tries to use goldenseal as a diaphoretic to reduce a fever. A diaphoretic is something that causes the body to sweat. This is a natural process that the body uses to control a fever among other things. This event occurred at the Abbey of Ste. Anne de Beaupre (Outlander only, chapter 39).

GROUTWEED

Aegopodium podagraria

This plant has a couple of common names that include ground elder, snow-on-the-mountain, and Bishop's weed. The non-variegated-type is a very invasive hardy perennial. In doing so, only plant the variegated-type, which is hardy in USDA Plant Hardiness Zones 3a through 9a.

Groutweed will grow anywhere there is soil that is well-draining. When it comes to propagation, it can be started through division, simple layering or seed. If you choose to grow your groutweed through seed propagation, plant the seed outside either in the fall or after your local frost-free date. But due to this plant's invasive nature, the best propagation method is simply planting variegated plants in the grounds.

When planting groutweed plants, prepare the garden location, and mark off the 12 inch spacing per plant. Place your plant(s) in your selected locations. To keep the plant under control, deadhead the flowers. Also, consider planting it in a raised bed to control the spreading of the plant. As a last resort, spray an organic herbicide on the offshoots of the plant to reduce spreading through rhizomes.

In the storyline, Claire thinks that groutweed could be used as a treatment for hemorrhoids (Outlander only, chapter 1). As the name applies, this herb has been used to treat gout along with other rheumatic diseases, which include autoimmune disorders.

Yes, Claire was right in believing that groutweed could be used to treat hemorrhoids. It is also used as a treatment for kidney, bladder, and intestinal issues.

HOREHOUND

Marrubium vulgare

The history of horehound is as unique as the uses for this herb mentioned in the series of books and STARZ show. In the series, Claire believes that horehound can be used to treat Jamie's hangover (Dragonfly in Amber, chapter 6). Claire also feels that steeping horehound, anise angelica, and peppermint together in a tea could be a treatment for Duncan Innes's constipation (Voyager, chapter 43). She also considers mixing horehound with fennel as a treatment for phantom limb pain, which Duncan Innes is suffering from (Voyager, chapter 43).

To diverge from the uses described in the books, and STARZ series, horehound is labeled as one of the five plants mentioned in the Seder feast of the Jewish Passover Celebration. When this herb is consumed during this feast, it is to remind those celebrating the bitterness of captivity that the Jewish people suffered while in Egypt. Some etymologists believe that the Latin name (*Marrubium)* actual comes from the Hebrew word marror, which translated means "bitter juice."

During the Middle Ages, horehound was used as a treatment for animal bits, and vegetable poisonings but there is no factual evidence that it works. In the past, it was also used to clear the respiratory system, and today it is believed to have some benefit since it thins out the mucus secretions. Beyond this use, horehound treats digestive issues, such as constipation, bloating, and even indigestion. Some individual even apply it to the skin as an ointment to treat minor skin damage, and wounds.

While the use of horehound as a way of treating constipation is straightforward, the other ailments that Claire uses this herb for are not that clear-cut. One explanation for the use as a hangover treatment and phantom limb pain comes from fact that this herb's use includes decreasing inflammation in the body, and a spasm reducer. This latter treatment could have given Duncan Innes relief from the phantom limb.

Horehound is a hardy perennial in USDA Plant Hardiness Zones 4 through 8. Believe it or not, horehound is in the mint family, and you know what that means. It can be invasive. There are several reasons why it has an invasive nature. First, it is not picky about the soil. As long as it is well-draining, life is good. One limiting factor though is the sun. Horehound does require direct sunlight.

Beyond that, this herb does well directly seeding into the prepared garden space after your local frost-free date. To hold the seed down, top off with ¼ inch of soil and water in until the soil is evenly moist. Continue to keep the soil moist. In two to three weeks, you will see your horehounds seeds germinate. Once they have their second set of leaves, thin them out so that there is 12 inches between each plant. Do not add any additional water. Once horehound is established, it likes to dry out a bit.

When it comes to caring for your horehound, the process is simple. Cut your horehound 1/3 down. After that first year, cut the horehound down to four-inches from the ground. This will encourage new growth on plant along with several flushes that you can harvest through the growing season. Another plus is the fact that frequent harvesting will reduce the chances of blooms, which would contain seed that would spread the plant more.

HYSSOP

Hyssopus officinalis

This perennial herb has a large range, which includes USDA Plant Hardiness Zones 3 through 9. The only true limiting factor of this plant is its sunlight requirement. Growing this herb in full sun is best but it can tolerate partial shade.

When it comes to the soil, it needs to be well-draining. One of the unique characteristics of this plant is the fact that it is also drought tolerant.

Propagating this perennial herb occurs through seed, cuttings and division. Planting the seeds can occur indoors or out. If you start your seeds inside, make sure to start six to eight weeks prior to your local frost-free date. Starting your seeds outside should start in late fall and in a cold frame. If you do not have a cold frame, it is still worth planting the seeds in the garden space in the spring. The reason for this is the fact that hyssop reseeds easily. Growing your seeds outside will produce stronger plants.

Despite where you start your seeds, simply add well-seasoned compost to your container or garden space. Once that is done, sprinkle the seed on the prepared planting medium surface and cover with ¼ inch of soil. Mist with water until the soil is evenly moist. If using a container, moisten the soil before planting.

Place the pot on a sunny windowsill and keep the soil evenly moist. At this point, you will need to wait 14 to 21 days before your seeds start to germinate.

If you grow your hyssop indoors, harden the plants off two weeks prior to your local frost-free date. When ready to move to the garden space, plant the seedlings so that there is 6 to 12 inches between each plant.

Cuttings can be taken in late spring to early summer. The division of this plant occurs both in the fall and summer.

Because this plant is known to cause sweating when added to bathwater, this may be why Claire tried it as a fever reducer while at the Abbey of Ste. Anne de Beaupre (Outlander only, chapter 39). Another unique use for this herb comes from the pomander that Mr. Overhalt wears when on board the Porpoise. As the purser, he made contact with the passengers on the ship. Due to this contact Mr. Overhalt wore a pomander around his neck made with dried hyssop and sage to ward off the plague (Voyager, chapter 47).

No, there is no evidence that this was actually done by other people. The idea for this pomander may have derived from the fact that this herb is used to treat respiratory problems such as colds, coughs, and respiratory infections. Beyond that, skin conditions such as frostbite and irritations can be treated with this herb.

LAVENDER

Lavandula

There are several different species of lavender that have certain uses. ***Lavandula x intermedia Provence*** is grown for its aroma value in the perfume industry. *Lavandula spica,* which is grown in the garden as an ornament and as the aroma component for "oil of spike," or an aromatic vinegar, along with lavender water. *Lavandula officinalis* or *Lavandula augustfolia* is normally referred to as common or true lavender, but in many situations, the "true" lavender is contaminated with other species. An example of this is the *Lavandula hybrida.* This hybrid is a cross between *Lavandula augustfolia* and *Lavandula latifolia,* which is where lavadin oil is acquired.

The legendary use of lavender is not forgotten in the Outlander book series or STARZ show. The ability of lavender to calm the nerves is noted in the storyline (Dragonfly in Amber, chapter 20). This use is not a fable. Science has spent a lot of time proving this point. In several studies, it was learned that simply inhaling lavender oil increased alpha waves--which causes one to feel relaxed. The use of lavender to treat depression and anxiety may be why Claire chose to use dried lavender to help Jamie exorcises his demon--while he was healing from his sexual assault at the Abbey of Ste. Anne de Beaupre (Outlander, chapter 39).

Claire used lavender in a unique way that many people may have never heard of and that is as an edible. While it is not clear whether lavender and mint oil or dried plant material was mixed with a few drops of poppy syrup to help Alex Randall sleep, the just of this treatment was to aid in his slumber (Dragonfly in Amber, chapter 42).

Beyond using lavender as a calming agent, it can also be used to treat bloat, stimulate a menstrual cycle, reduce hair loss, and as a health benefiting spice.

When planning on growing lavender, check your local plant hardiness zone. Lavender is only hardy in USDA Plant Hardiness Zones 5a through 9b. This herb also requires a well-draining soil that is not too rich in organic matter. To improve drainage, mix in sand with the soil prior to planting. When it comes to sunlight, lavender really showcases itself in full sun but can tolerate some shade.

Lavender can be propagated in three ways, which includes seed, softwood and semi-hardwood cuttings.

While seed propagation may sound easy, it produces mixed results. In doing so, you need to plant more seed than you think you will need. Also, it takes 10 to 28 days and you will get less than a 50 percent germination rate. Some individuals have found that exposing the seed to the cold (scarification) can sometimes increase the germination rate slightly.

To plant the seed, start off with preparing the pot but to increase the survival rate of the seedlings, use peat pots. This type of container will allow you to transplant the seedlings into their permanent location without disturbing the roots. Once you have your chosen container, fill with a light mix or seed starting medium that has been moistened. Next, plant one to two seeds per container. Mist the containers after they have all been filled, and place on a sunny windowsill in a warm room.

When it comes to propagating lavender through a softwood cutting or tip, you will first need to take a three to four-inch cut of new growth in the early spring or autumn. Keep in mind that spring cuttings root faster. This technique is great one to use when your prune back your lavender or shape it.

The second type of cutting is the semi-hardwood cuttings. This type of cutting starts off with a side shoot that is cut but pulled down along the stem so that there is some wood left on the end or heel.

Both of types of cuttings will need the bottom third of the leaves removed, the cut end dipped into rooting hormone, and the treated cut placed in a container of moistened sand. Place the container of cuttings in an area that receives filtered sunlight. Keep the sand evenly moist, and in about two weeks your cuttings will have rooted. At that point, you will need to transplant them into individual pots until they are large enough to plant in the garden.

Lavender requires a well-draining soil in a very sunny location. This perennial shrub should be spaced 12 to 18 inches apart. The determining space is dependent on the use, which can range from a hedge to a specimen plant and even a companion in the flower garden. To grow stronger plants, sprinkle bone-meal or any high phosphorus fertilizer around each one in the fall. While you can mix this into the soil, I have found that this can be a mistake. You can easily damage the roots of this herb. The best approach is to simply allow the rain to carry the phosphorus rich fertilizer down through the soil.

MADDER ROOT

Rubia tinctoria

This plant's USDA Plant Hardiness Zones range from 6a to 10b. Not a lot of information of growing the plant exists, but in general, the steps involved start off with planting fresh seeds in individual pots that have been filled with fresh compost. Water the seeds in and keep the soil moist. Place the planted containers in a location that receives partial shade to full shade.

Once you see the madder root begin to spread, this is an indication that the roots are established. At this point you can plant your madder root in your shady garden space and continue to water as needed to keep the soil moist at all times. If you let the soil dry out, your madder root seedlings will die.

Another form of propagation that works for madder root is taking a cutting. Regardless of which technique you choose, make sure you want madder root. Due to its creeping nature, this plant grows on everything and can become a problem.

The color of madder root has made this plant a favorite when it comes to dying clothing. For this to happen, the fluid from the common madder is collected. The pigment from this liquid is called rose madder. Taking advantage of this characteristic, Claire made a rose madder fluid that she gave to Murtagh to not only mimic the symptoms of a fever but also blood in the urine (Dragonfly in Amber, chapter 23). Mimicking these symptoms helped convince people that smallpox had resurfaced.

When madder root is applied to the skin, it has been noted to aid in wound healing. Taken by mouth, this plant has been known to treat kidney stones, menstrual problems, blood disorder, and even as a sexual stimulate.

MALLOW ROOT

Althaea officinalis

While Geillis may have given her husband mallow root for his farting (Outlander only, chapter 9), there is no indication that it is used for this specific issue. Instead, mallow leaf and root is used in the treatment of inflammation, which includes the respiratory system and intestinal tract lining. When one is talking about the respiratory system, a dry cough is the issue. As Claire was advised by Grannie McNab, consuming mallow root treats a cough (Outlander only, chapter 28).

Mallow root also has a role in skin care. When a poultice of mallow root and leaves is created, it treats simple aliments such as insect bites to infection filled pockets, and even burns.

The value of this plant in herbal medicine can be found in its genus name. The Greek term "altho" translated means "to cure," which is why Greek healers valued this plant so much.

An interesting note to where Claire found mallow root growing, which was by the millpond close to Lallybroch (Outlander only, chapter 28). What is interesting is the fact that mallow root was introduced to Scotland even though it was noted to be growing in Europe from Denmark southward.

The USDA Plant Hardiness Zones for this perennial include areas in 3 through 9. Beyond that, this plant needs a soil that remains wet all the time. When trying to picture this environment, picture a bog or pond. Mallow root loves areas that receive mixed amounts of sunlight and shade but if this is not possible, it can survive in full sun and shade.

Planting the mallow root begins with exposing the seeds to cold by first adding moist soil to a sealable bag and then sprinkling seeds inside. Place the bag in the refrigerator for three to four weeks. This should be done so that when your cold exposure time is up, you have six to eight weeks before your local frost-free date.

Keep an eye on your seeds in the refrigerator. If you see seeds starting to germinate, transplant them into individual pots that have been filled with an all-purpose potting soil. Place the planted pots on a sunny windowsill and continue to keep the soil moist. Do not let the soil dry out. If this happens, your seedlings will die.

Two weeks prior to your local frost-free date, place them outside to harden them off.

If you do not want to go through the "chilling" process, plan on planting your seeds in late summer to early fall. Regardless of when you plan on seeding patience is the key. Mallow roots seeds can take between 14 and 21 days to germinate.

When planting in the garden, make sure to give the plants room, which means spacing them 12 inches apart.

Other forms of propagation that works when it comes to mallow root include cuttings, and digging up side shoots.

MARJORAM

Origanum majorana

An interesting story about marjoram is centered on the Greek goddess Aphrodite. In the story, Aphrodite who was the goddess of love, grew marjoram in her garden. Because of this relationship with the goddess of love, marjoram has been used in many love potions and in woven garlands. These garlands were worn by both the bride and groom.

In ancient times, it was not uncommon to find people putting a little marjoram under their pillow at night. It was believed that sleeping on this herb would encourage one to have dreams of true love. Before the Middle Ages, a new belief arose. It was believed that if you planted this herb on top of a loved ones grave, then happiness would be brought forth for the departed one.

The role that marjoram plays in the story comes from a simple description that Geillie's clothing had an aroma of marjoram (Outlander, chapter 24).

Beyond adding flavor to dishes, marjoram has been taken for a vast number of purposes, which span from treating colds to stomachaches and reducing the symptoms brought on by menopause. It is sometimes also used as a heart tonic to improve blood circulation, and an herbal version of a water pill.

When it comes to growing marjoram, it is considered a perennial but it can be grown as a tender perennial in USDA Plant Hardiness Zones 6b through 11. The most likely way you will propagate your marjoram is through seed but it can also be divided, and through both soft-and semi-hardwood cuttings.

If you live in any of the USDA Plant Hardiness Zones mentioned above, you can seed directly into the prepared garden space but for the rest of us, the seeds will need to be started six weeks prior to your local frost-free date.

To begin this process, calculate your planting date with calendar. Next, as the planting date get nearer, clean and sterilize the container. Once that is done, fill the prepared container with a well-draining, all-purpose potting soil mix. Add water to the soil until you see moisture come out the bottom of the container. Now you are ready to plant your marjoram seeds.

You may notice that the seeds of this herb are tiny and only need to be sprinkled on the dampened soil surface. After all the seeds have been planted, mist the soil again and place on a sunny windowsill that is south facing. Continue to monitor the soil moisture and in 8 to 14 days you will see seedlings begin to appear. Keep in mind that germination rate is around 50 percent and growth of the seedlings is slow and you will need to be patient.

Monitor soil moisture and two weeks prior to your local frost-free date harden the seedlings off. Now you are ready to move your herb to a container garden with basil or in the herb garden.

Marjoram likes a well-draining soil that has lots of organic matter. The light requirement is full sun.

When planting your marjoram in the ground, make sure you give it the space it needs. If you plant single plants, space them out six to eight. Another approach is to plant your marjoram in clumps. If this is more to your liking, space out a clump of two to three plants so that there is 12 to 14 inches of space separating the clumps.

To encourage the marjoram to branch out, pinch the tips of the herb back often. Feed your marjoram monthly with a balanced, organic fertilizer.

Due to the poor germination rate of marjoram seeds, most plants purchased at the local garden store are grown from cuttings. The simplest way to take a cutting of marjoram begins in the middle of summer. Examine your marjoram plant and select the healthiest stems that have no buds. Cut these stems three inches long and remove the lower leaves. Dip each cutting in a rooting hormone and place in your moistened planting medium. After all your cuttings have been planted, move your cuttings to a shady location. Keep the soil evenly moist and in three weeks your cuttings will have developed strong roots. Once that has happened, transplant your cuttings into individual six-inch pots.

MEADOWSWEET/DROPWORT

Filipendula ulmaria

The only mention of meadowsweet in the series is that it was sighted growing in the Highlands (Outlander, chapter 17). But a common name for meadowsweet is dropwort. In some writings, this herb is referred to as dropwort meadowsweet. While the above notation of where the term "meadowsweet" is mentioned in the storyline, the alternative name is used by Claire when she finds dropwort growing nearby Lallybroch's millpond (Outlander only, chapter 17). While the discussion of this herb stops here, dropwort meadowsweet has a unique history.

Felix Hoffmen, a chemist by trade discovered that a byproduct produced by the meadowsweet plant contained salicylic acid in 1897. During this time period, the name for meadowsweet was Spiraea. The drug aspirin that would be derived from this plant in turn got its name from the "a," which came from acetylic acid and "spir" from Spiraea.

Beyond pain relief and inflammation, meadowsweet is noted to treat colds and other respiratory problem due to its ability to reduce mucus.

This herb is a perennial in USDA Plant Hardiness Zones 3 through 7. It loves to grow in sunny locations along creeks or ponds. If you do not have this ideal location, do not think you cannot grow this herb. Meadowsweet can survive in partial shade. But the real limiting factor is the soil, which needs to be moist and full of organic material.

When it comes to propagating the meadowsweet, it can be done through seed and division. If you have meadowsweet or your gardening friend is willing to share, harvest the seeds as soon as they are ripe in the fall. If your area receives cold temperature during the winter, you can directly seed into the garden space. On the other hand, if you have bought your seeds or you want to store them, you will need to place them in the refrigerator for three months prior to planting.

Once the three months are up, your seeds are ready to plant. This step is simple and requires one to clean and sterilize a container that is at least four-inches deep. Next, fill with new or sterilized growing medium, which can be compost or all-purpose potting soil. Sprinkle the seeds on to and lightly cover with perlite. Mist the perlite with water. The reason for using perlite is two-fold for these seeds. One, since this plant loves moisture, perlite absorbs the water and keeps it around the seed. This prevents the seed from drying out and dying. The second reason is the fact that meadowsweet seeds require light to germinate. The porous nature of perlite allows the light to reach the seed.

Place the planted container in a sunny window and monitor the soil moisture by testing it with your finger. Water as needed and be patient. Meadowsweet can take up to three months to germinate.

Continue to monitor soil moisture and start the hardening off process two weeks prior to your local frost-free date.

When it comes to the second form of propagation division, this should occur every three to four years. The trick to this approach is to make sure that every divided piece has at least one rhizome.

To keep meadowsweet looking its best, lay down a thick layer of well-seasoned compost and prune it back to the ground in the fall. This latter task will encourage young growth. Since meadowsweet likes damp soil, consider adding two to three inches of mulch every year to control weeds and preserve soil moisture.

An interesting note about this herb, it happened to be one of Queen Elizabeth I's favorite herbs to strew. Strewing consists of placing aromatic herbs in a container with water, heating it up to release the aroma. While the aroma of many herbs prepared this way gave people headaches. Meadowsweet was found not to produce this effect. Because of this, meadowsweet was used to perfume wedding events and later on developed the nickname "bridewort."

MINT

Mentha

When it comes to mint, the general term describes type of perennial plant that has a telltale characteristic of a square stem. This plant, in general, is hardy in USDA Plant Hardiness Zones 3 through 8. But before you go out and buy a lot of mint, check the hardiness of each variety you plan on planting.

Yes, you can get mint seed but the germination rate is unpredictable. The best approach comes from planting plants. Since mint's invasive nature makes it a nuisance, make sure you really want mint in the garden and/or check with your gardening friends for mint plants. I promise you, if they have mint they will be grateful to give you a start.

Believe it or not, mint grows anywhere. It prefers a partially shady location but will grow in full sun. The soil needs to be moist but well-draining. To keep your mint under control, consider planting it in bottomless pots that are 15 inches deep. Once planted, dig a hole in your garden space and bury the pot to the point that only one to inches stick above the ground. Another approach consists of planting your mint in clay chimney flue that has been cut into 12 to 15 inches long. When this cut chimney flue is planted it can be left on the soil's surface or buried down 2 to 4 inches. Regardless of which approach you pick, digging up the mint and dividing it will need to occur every two to three years.

If you are looking for a simpler way to plant your mint, just plant it in a deep container and keep above ground.

To keep mint looking its best, harvest leaves by cutting the stems often. Remove any flowers once they appear. Cut down to ground level in the fall.

The fresh smell of mint enveloped Geilles's clothes (Outlander, chapter 17). When Alex Randall had a hard time sleeping, Claire treated him with poppy syrup steeped with mint, and lavender (Dragonfly in Amber, chapter 42).

Mint contains an anti-inflammatory and antioxidant called rosmarinic acid. In recent studies, this chemical is showing process as an alternative treatment to seasonal allergies. Colds, and the symptoms associated with this aliment--along with upset stomachs--have been treated with mint leaves steeped in water or tea. Chewing the leaves provide oral care. While these uses sound normal, a published study done in 2007 showed that rubbing the nipples of nursing mother with peppermint water reduces the cracking of the nipples. All of these uses plus more is why Claire included this on her list of herbs she added to her medical kit. This medical kit would be carried on her voyage to the West Indies when she was looking for Ian (Voyager, chapter 40).

MULLEIN

Verbascum thapsus

In the Outlander series, this herb is mentioned in the book Dragonfly in Amber Chapter 2. Mullein's role was to act as toilet paper but in real life, it acts as so much more.

This biennial's flexibility can be found in the numerous names it goes by, which includes grandmother's flannel, shepherd's club, velvet dock, blanket herb, candlewick plant, hag's taper, and woolen rag paper.

In the past, this herb has been used for many purposes beyond toilet paper. Mullein is known to put moisture back into the respiratory tract and in doing so has been used to treat colds, and asthma. This herb also has a calming effect on both the mind and body. Due to this characteristic, it was also used to treat insomminia, earaches, and sore throats. While these uses are somewhat common, there are two unique functions that this herb played a part in. The first one was as a wick for candles since the leaves burn easily. The second odd use of mullein came into play as part of spell. The use of the herb in this capacity was viewed to chase away evil spirits.

When it comes to growing mullein, you may find that you already have some growing in your local area. It is considered to be a weed growing along roadsides and can commonly be found in Europe to Asia through the United States.

While you may think that there is only one variety, this is not true even though the most common type is referred to as Common Mullein. The remaining varieties include Olympic Mullein, Greek Mullein, White Nettled-Leaf Mullein, 'Summer Sorbet' Mullein, and 'Southern Charm' Mullein. Depending on the type, the blooms of these latter varieties can range from yellow, white, lavender, and rose.

Mullein is a pretty easy going herb that loves the sun and can be found growing happily in USDA Plant Hardiness Zones 3 through 9. As a matter of fact, it really thrives when it receives 8 to 10 hours of full sun. It also is not picky about its soil and really prefers poor soil but can tolerate any type of planting medium.

When it comes to planting mullein seeds, they require a little extra care. What this means is that the seeds themselves need to be cold stratified to germinate, but do not just put your seeds in the refrigerator. In the early spring, pull out your planting supplies. Using a 2-inch pot, lay one seed down on top of the soil and gently push down. Since this seed needs sunlight to germinate, you do not want to completely cover the seed. The best approach is to sprinkle a very fine layer of vermiculite on top of the seed. Once that is done, cover the top with clear plastic wrap. This cover will help keep the soil moist. Place in the refrigerator for 30 days.

After the cold stratification time period has passed, take out of the refrigerator, remove the plastic wrap, and place on a sunny windowsill. In 7 to 21 days, you will begin to see growth. Monitor soil moisture and once the mullein has produced its second set of leaves, you are ready to plant outside.

When it comes to planting mullein outside, make sure to space the plants 16 inches apart.

If you really do not want to start mullein indoors, you can direct seed this plant in the late summer to fall. When choosing this approach, make sure to cover the seed with 3/8 inch of soil and a layer of mulch. Doing this step will keep the seed away from the birds.

Planting mullein alone looks beautiful but if you really want to highlight the natural characteristics of this plant, consider planting with daylilies, yarrow, and miscanthus.

MUSTARD

Brassica

When it comes to mustard, you have the "green" or foliage and the seed. As a "cool season" green, the foliage of the mustard plant, when sautéed with other greens, makes a wonderful dish. While it may be assumed that there is only one type of seed, this would be incorrect. Mustard seed comes in both white and black. Each color posses its own therapeutic purposes.

Claire is told that mustard seed is good for the kidneys by Mr. Willoughby (Voyager, chapter 4). There is no indication as to which mustard seed Mr. Willoughby is recommending.

When one consumes white mustard seed, the aliments that it treats include; reducing water weight, increasing the appetite, and as a treatment by which to "cleanse the voice." Some individuals apply the white mustard seed to the chest to treat colds, and coughs. Another use comes from using this mustard seed in a paste, putting it on a cloth, and applying it to areas of the body where pain exists (mustard plaster).

A rather unique use of white mustard seed comes when it is added to a bath. Soaking in this mustard water gives some type of relief to those suffering from paralysis.

Black mustard seed is also used for the same aliments as the white mustard. Due to the flavor of the black mustard greens, these greens are selected for growing in vegetable gardens. Since it is noted that mustard grew in the herb garden at Castle Leoch, it's assumed that both are possible (Cross Stitch only, Chapter 6).

Growing mustard for greens and/or seed, starts off with pulling out the calendar. Since mustard is a cool season or Cole crop, it likes the weather below 75 degrees Fahrenheit. As a matter of fact, to get the most out of your mustard, start your plantings four to six weeks prior to your local frost-free date.

Once you have the date, you will want to prepare the garden space or container for the mustard. This step begins with site location. During the cool temperatures of the season, mustard likes full sun. As the season progresses, partial shade becomes mustard's best friend. In doing so, pick a location that receives full sun to partial shade. Another approach consists of picking a location that is sunny and then adding shade when needed.

To complete the requirements of mustard, one must plant mustard seed in soil that is well-draining and full of organic matter.

Now that you have the date, and location, planting the mustard seed is simple. The first step begins with preparing the garden soil and adding additional organic matter such as well-seasoned compost and/or manure to the soil. Need more details, read up on this topic in the garden primer.

Once the garden is prepared, plant your seed to a depth of ¼ to ½ inch, and one inch apart. Cover the seeds with a dusting of soil. Going to plant your mustard in rows then make sure there is six to eight inches between rows. After the seeds have been planted, mist the soil and keep evenly moist. In 7 to 14 days, you will see signs of seed germination.

Repeat this process every two weeks if you desire a continuous supply of mustard throughout the spring months.

Container gardening of this plant, starts off with preparing the pot by cleaning and sterilizing it. Fill with a 50:50 mixture of all-purpose potting soil and well-seasoned compost and/or manure. Plant as described above.

Depending on the variety, thin your mustard so that there is 6 to 18 inches between plants.

Continue to water when needed. Keep in mind though that as the season warms up and approaches the 75 degree Fahrenheit, your mustard begins to "bolt." This term refers to the plant sending up a flower stalk. Once this happens, the greens become bitter. To keep your mustard from spreading everywhere, pull up the mustard plants that bolt.

Looking to get the most out of your garden space, consider planting English, and snap peas as companions.

NETTLES

Urtica dioica

Many times, the common name of a plant explains a characteristic of the plant and nettle is no different. When one hears the name nettle, it stills up a painful reminder of an event when one got into "stinging nettles." Stories are told about the pain from the exposure to the stinging nettle, which I am sure Hamish expressed when his pony bucked him off into a patch of nettles (Outlander, chapter 24). While exposing oneself to nettles is a silly mistake, the stinging nature of this plant made it a good choice for punishment of children and adults. In the storyline of series, Claire sleeps with King Louis XV to free Jamie. In response to hearing the news, Jamie asks Claire if he should lash her with stinging nettles due her indiscretion (Dragonfly in Amber, chapter 29). This nettle beating if it occurred would be painful and leave a rash. The skin's reaction to this plant is what Claire takes advantage of when she applied nettle juice to the skin to mimic the rash produced by smallpox (Dragonfly in Amber).

While there was no clear description of nettle juice being used, it is assumed that since the stinging hairs of the plant contain several chemical that cause discomfort so would the "juiced" plant.

The uses for stinging nettles go beyond a painful naissance or punishment. Drinking a tea made from steeped young nettles in the spring was an old time immunity booster. Applying stinging nettles to the skin reduces pain but scientists are not quite sure of the mechanism behind this effect. Some individuals believe that the sting from the stinging nettle changes the pain pathway of the area along with inflammation. Stinging nettles are also used in the treatment of urinary tract problems and infections.

Yes, nettles are a weed but if you want to grow them yourself, they are easy to propagate. This plant is a hardy perennial in USDA Plant Hardiness Zones 3 through 10. When it comes to location, nettles like a moist soil, which is why you can find them growing alongside streams. They prefer a rich soil in an area that receives partial shade. Having said all that, nettles will really pop up anywhere there is moist soil.

If you want to get a jump on the nettle season, you could start your seeds indoors but why would you take up the space. Instead, simply broadcast your seed in the prepared garden space in early spring or plant in rows one foot apart.

Since the seeds are small, gently tap the seeds down so that they make contact with the soil. Another approach is to cover them with less than ¼ inch of soil. Either way will work to hold the seed down but be careful not to cover the seed. Nettle seed needs light to germinate.

Another reason to directly seed your nettles in the early spring is due to the chance of a cold snap. It has been found that nettle seeds tend to germinate better when exposed to the cold.

Once the nettle seeds are planted, mist the area with water. In 10 to 14 days, you will see little green dots of growth. As soon as the seedlings are large enough to hold, thin them out to a spacing of 8 inches.

To keep nettles from taking over, follow these simple tips. Plant the nettles away from your vegetable, and herb garden. Also, keep it away from your landscaping. Next, pull up any uninvited nettle guests you find. To cut down on the reseeding, cut your nettles back in late summer. At this point, the leaves have become too tough eat.

NIGHTSHADE

Solanaceae

The term nightshade is a general one since there are over 2,500 shrubs, herbs, and even trees. While many of these plants are poisonous, some of them in this family show up in our vegetables gardens as tomatoes, pepper, potatoes. This plant also provides us with some enjoyment when tobacco is smoked.

While most plants in the nightshade family are poisonous, there is a pharmaceutical market for *Atropa belladonna*. The big growers that grow this particular nightshade include England, France, and even the United States. To meet the demand, wild populations are also harvested. There is no clear indication as to why type of nightshade is burned during the summoning spell that Geillie does with Claire (Outlander, chapter 24). With the limited information provided plus a spell that was found, the *Atropa belladonna* species is more likely the one burned. It is noted that a spell using *belladonna* can help heal one from the loss of a loved one.

As far as medical uses, some consume this plant to escape life through hallucinations and feelings of well being. Nightshade has also been used as a form of treatment for influenza, and swine flu along with diseases of the nerves.

It is not recommended that one grow any nightshade that has not been deemed safe to eat, such as vegetables. While you may feel that if this planting this plant in an obscure area of you yard will not be harmful, keep in mind that not only is it a killer of men but of beast.

In the United States, nightshade grows wild in shady areas of the forest in USDA Plant Hardiness Zones 5 through 9. An interesting note to this plant is the fact that many botanical gardens will grow this plant as a specimen to be studied.

The *Atropa belladonna* loves a most soil that is rich in organic material. It grows best in partial to fully shaded areas but will grow to a dwarfed size in full sun.

If you decide that you want to grow *Atropa belladonna,* the best approach is through seed or division. Either technique will require you to find a specimen and harvest the needed parts. Depending on the area by which you live, the scientific name may not be known to the local but another name for nightshade is Jimson weed.

NUTMEG

Myristica fragrans

This plant provides two spices for the price of one, so to speak. Nutmeg is the hard seed, which is covered by an aril. The brightly colored aril is what is dried and turned into mace.

Since flavoring for food on ships was limited, it was easy for Claire to bribe Mr. Murphy the cook on the Artemis with nutmeg (Voyager, chapter 41). It is not clear as to whether it was just the nut or the entire fruit, which would include nutmeg and mace.

If you live in USDA Plant Hardiness Zones 10 through 11 then you will have no problem growing this aromatic evergreen. On the other hand, if you do not recede in this limited area, you could have a challenge. The reason for this goes beyond the environment and has to do with the seed. Once the aril is removed, the seed's vitality decreases quickly. To achieve the highest level of success when it comes to this plant, you need to use seeds that have been harvested and process immediately off the tree.

When it comes to growing nutmeg, you need to start with the freshest seed. Before you throw it in a container, you need to prepare it. In nature, when the seed is ripe and ready to pick, the fruit will pop open exposing the bright red colored aril. This draws attention to wildlife who in turn removes the fleshy fruit covering along with the aril. Removing the aril allows the nutmeg seed to absorb water and start germinating. You can act as nature and remove the aril yourself but you will need to take precautions. First, pick a sharp knife and wipe it down with bleach or rubbing alcohol. This will sterilize the blade. Next, take a look at your fresh nutmeg. You will notice that the aril attaches itself to the "nut" in one area. This is the location by which you want to cut. After that is done, gently peel away the aril to expose the nutmeg nut.

To increase your chances of seed germination, soak your processed nutmeg seed in a bowl of clean water for 24 hours.

While you are waiting for your seed to take up water, prepare a five-inch pot by cleaning and sterilizing it. Place drainage material in the bottom and fill with a good all-purpose potting soil. To make watering easier, make sure to stop filling the container within one inch of the top.

After your nutmeg seed has soaked, remove it from the water and plant one inch deep into the soil. Water the container from the top until you see water come out the bottom of the pot. Place the planted container in a room that stays between 77 to 86 degrees Fahrenheit. Be patient at this point. The nutmeg seed takes up to a month to germinate. During this time, continue to water the pot and make sure that the soil remains moist but not soggy.

Once your nutmeg seed has germinated, continue to keep it in a warm place but expose it to four to six hours of sunlight. Mist the plant twice a day, check soil moisture, and rotate 180 degrees every other day.

As the nutmeg grows, it will eventually out grow its five-inch container. You can tell this by checking the bottom of the pot. If you see roots protruding from the holes in the bottom, then it is time to transplant. The process of transplanting begins with cleaning of the pot that is no more than two inches bigger. Since the five-inch pot is an old size, you can either go to a six or eight inch. If you decide on the latter, do not go beyond a 10-inch for the next transplant.

After you have the container, fill it as you did to start your seed. Continue to transplant as needed. Once the plant reaches the five gallon stage, it is time to plant outside. Planting your older seedling in the late spring in your landscaping will give it the best chance of survival. Also, make sure you give your plant its space. Nutmeg trees require 30 to 40 feet of growing room.

Both nutmeg and mace are used interchangeably it seems when it comes to medicine. These spices are known to kill bacteria and fungi. They are also used to relieve joint pain, and as a part of a cancer treatment. It has been found that giving a person nutmeg and/or mace has the potential to help with cases of diarrhea, and nausea. Another unique use for these two spices comes from them being used in a treatment to increase menstrual flow, which in some cases can bring on a miscarriage.

ORRIS ROOT

Iris florentina

While orris root is normally made up of three species of iris (*Iris florentina, Iris germanica,* and *Iris pallida),* the easiest two to grow at home are the *Iris florentiana* and *Iris pallida.* Due to the coloration of the blooms, some gardeners believe that the *Iris florentina* conforms better to the herb garden while the *Iris pallida* looks better in the perennial bed.

While you can start irises through seed, the easiest way is by planting its rhizomes. When using rhizomes, the first step of this process is site selection. The iris by which orris root comes from likes the soil a little dry. Irises also like a very sunny location. Without this requirement met, they will stop blooming.

To begin the planting process in USDA Plant Hardiness Zones 4 through 9, begins with preparing the soil in mid-to-late-summer. This is done by loosening up the soil down 12 to 15 inches. From here, mix in two to three inches of well-seasoned compost. Once that is done, smooth the soil over, and dig a hole that is 10-inches wide and four-inches deep. In the center of the hole, create a ridge by which you will sit your rhizome on with the roots hanging over each side of the ridge. Fill in the hole and slightly cover the top of the rhizome. You do not want to bury the rhizome like you would a bulb.

Repeat the process by planting individual rhizomes in groups of three, separated by one to two feet.

When finished planting, top dress the rhizomes with a low nitrogen fertilizer, and repeat again in the spring.

Once the planting is finished, water the rhizomes in to settle the soil.

Irises pretty much take care of themselves at this point but you will need to divide them every two to five years. Also, while you may be tempted to trim back the leaves after they have finished blooming, do not. The leaves are creating food by which the rhizome will store for next year.

In the Outlander book series and STARZ show, it is noted that Claire bought orris root while she was in Paris, France (Dragonfly in Amber, chapter15). Orris root, in the past, was a major component of face and foot powder along with dental creams. While the fresh rhizomes have no aroma, the dried rhizomes smell like violets. For this reason, orris root rhizomes have been used to scent sachet powders, add a violet aroma to soaps, and used as a freshener for wardrobes, linen closets, and storage chests. Whereas drying the rhizome may sound easy, it can take up to two years for the violet aroma to mature to the highest level.

Beyond the aroma, orris root is used as a "blood purifier," and "gland stimulator," which can increase the appetite, bile and kidney activity. It can also be used to treat pain, certain skin diseases, constipation, and even some cancers. When taken directly applied to the mouth, orris root can treat bad breath or put up the nose for the treatment of nasal polyps.

PARSLEY

Petroselinum crispum

The culinary delights of parsley are noted in the Outlander story and STARZ show. When the crew catches Mr. Murphy, the cook for the Artemis, a shark for dinner he walks away murmuring to himself about dried parsley (Voyager, chapter 44). Beyond the culinary use for parsley, it has been used to treat kidney stones, gas, constipation, jaundice, urinary tract infections, edema, and even the common cough. Some individuals rub parsley on the skin to treat bruises, insect bites, dry skin, and even to stimulate hair growth. While you may know about using parsley in culinary dishes, did you know that there is a reason for adding parsley to the side of your dinner plate beyond presentation? Well, parsley presented in this way serves two purposes. Yes, it does make the plate look beautiful but when eaten fresh, parsley freshens the breath.

When it comes to grow parsley, you will need to plan ahead to get the most from the plant. The first reason for this that while you can purchase parsley plants, it is just as easy to start from seed but the seed is slow to germinate. It can take up to three weeks for the seeds to break ground. In doing so, to get a jump on harvesting, plan on starting your seed 10 to 12 weeks prior to your local frost-free date. The second issue is one that not many people know. Parsley is actually a biennial that is grown as an annual. In doing so, while you can plant your seed in the garden, you will not maximize the plant's potential. If you have the time, start your parsley from seed. If harvesting the parsley is not the goal then simply use plants.

To speed up the germination of parsley seed, soak the seed overnight in water. While your seeds are soaking, prepare your container(s) by cleaning and sterilizing them. To save time, consider using peat pots. Regardless of which type of container you choose, fill with a moistened all-purpose potting soil mix or seed starting planting medium. If using peat pots, plant one seed per pot and cover with 1/8 inch of soil. If plastic pots or a flat is something you want to use, fill it up and sprinkle the seeds on top. Once all the seeds have been planted, mist the soil surface, and place your chosen container(s) on a sunny windowsill.

If you want to directly plant into your garden, make sure to remove all weeds and plant in rows. Due to the amount of time it takes for the seeds to germinate, it is important to be able to identify parsley seedlings. These little plants when they first appear look like little blades of grass.

Never let the soil dry out. A week prior to your local frost-free date, harden off the seedlings. While this process is going on, prepare the garden space, which needs to be weed free, well-draining, and in a sunny to partially shady area.

When it is time to plant your parsley in the garden space, set the plants so that they are 10 to 12 inches apart. To keep the soil moist and weeds at bay, top the soil with shredded leaves or grass clippings.

Feed your parsley twice through the growing season with a 5-10-5 organic fertilizer.

If you have no garden, do not worry. Parsley does very well in a container and can even be brought into the home prior to a killing frost. When using this approach, make sure to place the parsley in a sunny location, and feed it half strength liquid fertilizer every four weeks.

PELLITORY OF THE WALL

Parietaria officinalis

While it is not really noted as to why Claire adds this herb to her medical kit in Paris (Dragonfly in Amber, chapter 22), the aliments that this herb are used to treat explains why she included it. Pellitory of the Wall or lichwort has been known to be used as a treatment for fluid retention, kidney disorders, constipation, and coughing. To treat wounds and burns, pelitory of the wall is applied to the skin.

While there is no information on the USDA Plant Hardiness Zones, it can easily be found growing in cracks of walls or along stonewalls. As a matter of fact, the genus name *Parietaria* is derived from the Latin term *paries,* which means a wall.

When it comes to conditions by which this perennial can survive, one of the limiting factors is frost. Pellitory of the wall is not frost tolerant. The only true soil requirement is that it be well-draining. This plant can tolerate a dry soil or one that is moist but will not survive standing water or overly damp soil.

A sunny location or along the border of a forest where dabbles of light break through often is the solar requirement of this plant.

Propagation can be through seed or division. Seed propagation can occur in the spring or autumn. The seeds will need to be planted in a cold frame. While details on the depth could not be found, it is my educated guess that a surface broadcast would be fine. To protect the seed, cover with 1/8 inch of soil and water in.

As soon as the seedlings are large enough, plant in the garden. One note on the seeds though, to produce seeds you will need both a male and female plant. It is better to plant more seeds than you think you will need to increase the chances of getting both sexes.

If you do not want to use the cold frame approach, you can directly seed into the garden.

Division is simple. You find a friend with pelitory of the wall in the spring or autumn, dig the root mass up, divide it, and replant it. If the clump is really large, and your division is robust then you can simply plant it in the garden. If you have smaller clumps the best approach is to pot them up, and care for them until they are established in the container(s). Once that has happened, you can transplant them to the garden in the late spring to early summer.

PENNYROYAL

Mentha pulegium or Hedeoma pulegioides

The reason for the two different Latin names comes from the fact that there are two different types of pennyroyal. One is referred to the American Pennyroyal or squaw mint, mock pennyroyal and/or mosquito plant. The second pennyroyal is *Mentha pulegium* or European Pennyroyal. Since Davie Beaton made mention that he had used this herb to treat a thumb injury (Outlander, chapter 7), the latter variety will be discussed.

The European Pennyroyal is in the mint family and in doing so has the invasive nature that needs to be controlled by a barrier or container. When it comes to growing this in a permanent location outside, make sure you are in USDA Plant Hardiness Zones 5 through 9. If this does not apply to you, do not throw your gardening hands up. Pennyroyal is easily grown in containers.

Propagation of this plant can be from seed, cuttings, and division. Seeds can be started indoors or directly seeded into the ground. Pennyroyal seeds require light to germinate. In doing so, simply sprinkle the soil surface with the seeds and mist with water. Keep the soil evenly moist, and in two weeks or less you will see little green dots. These are the seedlings of the pennyroyal. As soon as they are large enough to handle, transplant into individual pots. One week prior to your local frost-free date, harden off the seedlings and plant in the proper garden space or container.

If you do not want to start your pennyroyal inside, plant it outside after your local frost-free date.

What is the proper outdoor environment for pennyroyal? Well, it really loves disturbed soil. While it is not picky about the soil type, it does grow best in soil that has a good amount of organic matter. When it comes to sunlight though, this requirement is a little tricky. No, it will not do well in full shade. This environment will cause the plant to grow spindly. On the other hand, full sun dries out the soil too much. The best environment for your pennyroyal is one that is full of sunlight but that has plants around this herb that can shade the soil. This type environment keeps the roots cool and the soil moist, which is what pennyroyal loves.

If you want to grow your pennyroyal in a container garden, consider using it as a trailer in a container garden design. Or, simply put it in a hanging basket.

When it comes to the other forms of propagation, the hardest part is finding a friend with this plant to get your first start. Pennyroyal cuttings should be taken in the spring. The process is easy. Clean your knife with rubbing alcohol, take a three to four-inch length cutting, remove 1/3 to 2/3 of the leaves from the bottom, and place in hole in moistened soil. Another approach is to water root the cutting by just placing it in a glass of water. The fine hairs along the stem will turn into roots very quickly. Once the roots have appeared, plant as described previously.

Division only requires digging up the whole plant every three years in the early spring. Once that is done, divide the root mass and replant.

To keep pennyroyal looking its best, pinch off the ends of the stems. This process will encourage the plant material to branch out and become bushy verses thin and spindly. If you prefer the latter, you can expect to grow a lean sub shrub.

As noted, pennyroyal in the story is used to treat a thumb injury (Outlander, chapter 7), which I am to assume means the skin was cut. In this example, pennyroyal when applied to the skin is used to kill germs. The aroma of this herb makes it one that in the past was used in perfume. Oil of pennyroyal and dried pennyroyal has been used to repel pests, such as fleas, and even summer insects when applied to the skin.

When consumed, this herb is noted to treat many different ailments but it is also very deadly. Ignoring this fact, pennyroyal has been used to treat kidney and gallbladder problems, intestinal issues, and even the common cold. The fact that consumption of this herb can stimulate menstruation has also been used to induce abortions.

PEPPERMINT

Mentha piperita

This herb has long been used to treat indigestion, which is why Geilles uses extract of peppermint to treat her husband's upset stomach (Outlander, chapter 9). Claire takes advantage of peppermint's ability to calm the stomach when she gives children who ate too much and/or too many sweets at the Gathering, peppermint syrup (Cross Stitch only, chapter 10). Claire treats Jamie's cold with a steeped pan of made peppermint and blackcurrant (Dragonfly in Amber, chapter 38). It is not clear as to whether Claire used this "tea" for Jamie to inhale the steam or to drink. Both ingredients can be drunk but some individuals do inhale peppermint oil as a treatment for colds and as a pain reliever. Lastly, when Duncan Innes complains about constipation, Claire prescribes a tea made from peppermint, horehound, anise, and angelica (Voyager, chapter 43).

Beyond the uses noted above, peppermint can be used to treat gas, bacterial and viral infections. When peppermint oil is applied to the skin, it repels mosquitoes, and can be used to treat allergic rashes.

Peppermint, as the Latin and common name apply, belongs to the mint family. What this means is that it can very easily become invasive. To prevent this, you can plant it in a bed that has a deep barrier that prevents the roots from spreading. This deep barrier needs to be between six to eight inches into the ground. Another choice is to plant your peppermint in a clay chimney flue liner or container.

Peppermint is a cross between water mint and spearmint. In doing so, this plant does not produce seed. To get started in growing peppermint will require one finding a friend with a plant or purchasing one.

If you can find that gardening friend, I promise you that this friend will love to share the mint. You can divide the plant in the spring or you can take cuttings. To do the latter, begins with wiping down a knife, going out to the garden and harvesting several three to four-inch long pieces. Once that is done, remove 1/3 to 2/3 of the leaves from the bottom and place in a glass of water. In a week or two, you will see roots beginning to appear on your mint. After your peppermint cuttings have rooted, plant in your chosen method.

Another propagation technique is to plant peppermint roots in the fall. You will need to plant your root cuttings two inches deep and space them out six to eight inches apart.

At this point, you may be wondering where to plant peppermint. Before I get to that, I have an ancient tale about peppermint that describes its ideal location. As the story goes, Pluto, who was the god who ruled over the underworld, met a young nymph named Menthe. After their first meeting, Pluto became engrossed in Menthe, which angered his wife. In response to Pluto's infatuation with Menthe, his wife had her turned into an herb. This herb could only be found in the damp shadows of the world, which is where you will find peppermint. This herb thrives in shady locations with damp soils.

To keep the mint looking its best, pinch off the ends of the stalks. This will help the plant develop a bushy appearance. While peppermint will really grow anywhere as long as the growing requirements are met, there are areas where winter temperatures can be a problem. In these areas, protect the peppermint roots by covering the plant with mulch before the winter wind blows. This technique will protect the roots from freezing and allow your perennial peppermint to reappear in the spring.

PLANTAIN

Plantago major

Walking through your yard, you may find plantain growing wild. In the United States, this plant goes by the name plantain in other countries plantago. The pleasure this plant brings comes from two factors. One, the leaves add a tasty treat to salads and tastes like spinach. Two, historically this plant found its way into treating conditions, which could range from snakebites to healing wounds. While it is not specified, what type of plantain Claire uses to treat a thumb infection but regardless several do treat skin infections (Cross Stitch only, chapter 9).

In the world of plantains there are four specific ones mentioned with a medical use. This includes the great, water, buckhorn, and black psyllium. Great plantain uses include treating bladder infections, bleeding hemorrhoids, and colds. The juice form the plantain can also be applied to the skin for many different ailments. Appling the juice of the plantain (plantago) to burns as Claire mentioned to Jamie (Voyager, chapter 27), may reduce the swelling and pain of a burn while killing germs.

Some individuals use water plantain to treat bladder and urinary tract infection. But this is not recommended due to the lack of research. Buckhorn plantain soothes the respiratory system and skin by reducing swelling and pain.

Black psyllium's common name is plantain. When consuming the seeds of this plant, relief from constipation can occur. Irritable bowel syndrome and diarrhea treatments can also contain these seeds.

Since this plant grows in lawns easily, planting it for domestication starts off with confinement. Create a seedbed or container and sprinkle your seed on the soil surface and dust with soil. Mist the soil until evenly moist. In 7 to 14 days, you will see your seeds germinating. For the best germination rate, make sure that the planted area receives full sun to partial shade.

While this perennial herb survives in USDA Plant Hardiness Zones 3 through 9, you can grow this plant indoors for year-round pleasure. To do this, follow the directions above with one difference. You are going to make a planting medium that consists of four parts well seasoned compost to one part sand. Mix well, fill container, and plant.

PURSLANE

Portulaca oleracea

The purslane emerging from the cracks of your sidewalk belong to the same ones in the herb garden at Castle Leoch (Outlander only, chapter 6). This plant goes by several names such as hogweed, pigweed, common purslane, and green purslane. In traditional Chinese medicine, purslane goes by the name Ma Chi Xian, which translated means "horse tooth amaranth.

Some refer to this plant as a succulent herb due to its juicy or succulent leaves. The easy and flexibility of this plant makes it a favorite edible weed but growing it yourself will not be a challenge.

While this plant grows anywhere, one requirement is that the growing season lasts for at least two months. It does its best in sunny locations where the soil drains well but frankly, it will pop up anywhere there is soil.

The planting process starts off with simply loosing up the garden soil, and sprinkling the seed. The small seed only needs a gently misting at this point.

If you do not want to plant purslane in the ground, pull out a container, fill with soil, and sprinkle the surface with seeds.

A constant supply of purslane will be yours if you do one or both of these things. One, cut the purslane back for a second round of this herb prior to a killing frost. The second approach consists of planting seed every six weeks.

Uses for purslane come from containing omega 3 fatty acids, antioxidants along with other vitamins and minerals. Some aliments that purslane can possibly effect include asthma, type 2 diabetes, and unusual abdominal bleeding.

ROSEMARY

Rosmarinus officinalis

Rosemary is a perennial herb that is also an evergreen shrub. It thrives in USDA Plant Hardiness Zones 7a to 10b. While you can grow it in areas less than 7, you will only be able to grow it as an annual. You can transplant your rosemary and move it indoors but this herb typical is a challenge to grow indoors.

Another issue with rosemary, is the fact that the germination rate of the seeds tends to be unpredictable. You also need to set aside three months prior to your local frost-free date to start your seed. While this may not be a challenge you want to take, I have had success in growing rosemary from seed. Whilst the germination rate was very poor, I do recommend you giving it a try.

As stated above, you will need to count back three months from your local frost-free date to get your planting schedule. Once you have that you can prepare to plant by cleaning and sterilizing your container. A shallow one is just fine since you are simply starting your seeds.

One trick I have learned when it comes to rosemary seed is to soak the seed prior to planting. To get the best results, soak your seed four to six hours before you plant your seed.

While your rosemary seeds are soaking, fill your container with a light potting soil, sand, perlite or vermiculite. Sprinkle the seed on top and barely cover the seed with your chosen planting medium. Mist with water until the planting medium is evenly moist. Cover the container with a glass pane or clear plastic wrap. If using the latter, make sure to secure it to the container. Place the planted container in a warm location.

Once you see little green dots appear, remove the cover of glass or plastic and move the potted container to a sunny location. Continue to monitor the soil moisture. The key at this point is to not let the soil dry out but do not let it stay wet.

After the seeds have reached three inches in height, you can transplant them into the garden space if your frost-free date has passed. If the environmental conditions are not right, transplant the rosemary seedlings into individual pots that have been filled with well-draining soil. Place in a warm and sunny location.

If growing rosemary from seed is not something you want to do then you will need to either buy a plant or take a cutting. While you may think that you can only get a cutting from a plant, this is not true. You can find suitable cuttings in your local grocery store by visiting the produce section. In this area, you can find fresh herbs by which starts can be harvested. When using this approach, make sure the fresh rosemary is as fresh as possible.

Whether you get your cutting from the evergreen shrub or you produce section, the key to success is cutting new growth. You will need a four to six-inch cutting. Once you have your cutting, remove all the leaves except four to six on the very top. Cut the cutting again at an angle at a leaf node or where the leaf attaches to the stem. Dip the cut end into a rooting hormone and place in a container that is filled with equal parts of potting compost, sand, and perlite or vermiculite. When putting your cutting in the container, make sure that the stem goes down through the soil up to but not touching the lower leaves of the cutting. If the lower leaves are touching the soil, remove and repeat. Letting leaves touch the soil will cause rotting and possibly the loss of the cutting.

After all the cuttings have been taken, water in the cuttings, and place a clear plastic bag around the cuttings. This will make a "greenhouse" by which the cutting will remain moist but not wet. Place in a warm location away from direct sunlight. In a few weeks, open up the plastic bag and tug on cuttings. If you feel resistance, the cuttings have rooted and can either be planted in the garden or in containers.

While you can grow rosemary in a container, keep in mind that it can reach three to four feet in height and up to four feet in diameter. If you have the space, I would recommend growing it in your garden or finding the low growing variety.

Rosemary loves a well-draining soil that is located in a sunny location but can tolerate some shade. Keep in mind though, the shadier the location, the more your rosemary will grow spindly.

To keep your rosemary healthy and producing new shoots, prune back one-third. Do not remove anymore until this new growth has replaced what was removed.

While rosemary is a little flexible on the amount of sunlight it receives, the one thing it is not is moisture. Overwatering rosemary is one of the number one killers of this plant. It is fine to let the soil dry out, and as a matter of fact, this herb does very well in xeriscaping projects.

If planting rosemary in an herb garden, avoid planting it near basil, but sage and thyme make good neighbors for this herb.

Claire found this herb in Davie Beaton's surgery while she was at Castle Leoch (Outlander, chapter 7). When Claire needed to mimic the flushing and feverish symptoms of smallpox, she tried rubbing rosemary essence on the skin (Dragonfly in Amber, chapter 23). This latter use is not too far from accounted uses of oil of rosemary. When applied to skin it irritates the area and improves blood circulation. This irritation is what Claire was hoping to create. Since application of this oil irritates the skin, it is used on the scalp to aid in hair growth or preventing baldness. It is also used as an insect repellent, wound treatment, and even added to a bath in balneotherapy.

Beyond culinary delights, rosemary as a treatment for digestive problems, gout, high blood pressure, and even age-related memory loss.

ROSEROOT

Rhodiola rosea

Roseroot belongs to the stonecrop family and grows wild in Finland. The real limiting factor of this plant consists of the temperature. Roseroot needs it cool during some time of its growing cycle. For the seeds of this perennial to germinate, the temperature needs to drop down to at least 32 degrees Fahrenheit. This equates out to a USDA Plant Hardiness Zones 1a to 10a.

When it comes to propagating roseroot, the easiest way is through seed. The process of this form of propagation begins with counting back 12 to 16 weeks from your local frost-free date. Next, moisten a small amount of soil and put in a sealable plastic bag. Sprinkle the seed inside this bag, shake and close. Place your planted bag in the refrigerator for six weeks.

Once the chilling period passes, remove the seeds and place them in a flat filled with moistened, all-purpose potting soil. Sprinkle the seeds on top of this soil and mist with water. Place the planted flat in a room that is kept around 50 degrees Fahrenheit. The best sunlight at this stage is indirect.

Continue to monitor soil moisture and only water by misting. This is due to the small size of the seed. In two to four weeks the roseroot seeds will break ground.

Once the seedlings have their second set of leaves, transplant into individual pots but be careful. Damaging the roots at this stage can occur easily. Move the transplants to a sunny location once the stalks start to appear, which will take one to two months from the time of germination.

Harden off the seedlings two weeks prior to your local frost-free date. When moving to the garden, pick a sunny location with well-draining soil.

Roseroot's role in the story comes from Geillis who told Claire that it could grow a wart on anyone's nose (Cross Stitch only, chapter 9). While no such evidence for this claim appeared, the University of Pennsylvania tested what our ancestors used it for, which was for depression and sluggishness. Roseroot shows promise in treating depression, or better yet, increasing the brain chemicals that make us feel good.

SAFFRON

Crocus sativus

The historical use of saffron as a spice is demonstrated in two situations that take place in the Outlander book series and STARZ show. As a treat, Geillie brings Mrs. Fitz saffron from Spain (Outlander, chapter 24). To get better tasting food while on the Artemis, Claire bribes the cook with several different spices including saffron (Voyager, chapter 41).

In today's time, saffron is still a valuable and expensive herb. The reason is two-fold. First, while saffron is easy to grow, it is labor intensive to harvest. The second reason is the small amount that is produced by each flower. Believe it or not, saffron is actually the three red stigmas that are in the center of each bloom. These red stigmas can be harvested and used fresh or dried. The latter is what is found in spice isle.

To really make it worth your while, it is a good idea to grow at least 50 corms, which will require a two-foot by five-foot space. Also, for the saffron bulbs to survive in the ground, you will need to live in USDA Plant Hardiness Zones 6 thorough 9. But if you do not have this space, you can grow your saffron corms in a container and even indoors if needed.

If you are going to grow saffron bulbs in the ground, you will first need the proper location and then prepare it early. The best location for saffron corms is in a well-draining soil that is in full sun. If you have high clay content in your soil, do not waste your time planting saffron bulbs in this soil. They will simply rot. Your time would be better spent planting them in a container.

Once you have found the ideal soil that meets the sunlight requirement, remove all plant material. Mix in a good amount of well seasoned compost. Loosen the soil down eight inches. All of this should be down in the late spring. While you are waiting for your bulbs to arrive, keep the area weed free.

Saffron corms do not last very long outside of the soil. In doing so, plant them as soon as they arrive. Since this bulb is autumn flowering, the planting period should be from June to August.

When it comes time for planting, pull out your ruler, and mark off every six inches with powdered milk. At each one of these marks, plant a bulb three inches down. After all the bulbs have been planted, water in the soil.

The first year of growth normally does not produce flowers but do not be alarmed. They will send up leaves that look like little blades of grass.

To aid in weed control, consider planting a summer blooming annual. This will cover the ground, provide color while reducing the number of weeds that popup. Once the annual is done, simply pull it up to reveal the grass-like leaves. From the second year on, the grass-like leaves will be topped with purple blooms.

Growing saffron in a container is not difficult. The key is top the drainage material with well-draining soil mixed with seasoned compost. Place the container in a sunny location. Since the saffron is in a container, you will need to monitor the soil moisture, and water when needed.

Prior to a killing frost, bring in your saffron crocus, and put it in a cool room where they can get four to six hours of sunlight. Water your saffron crocus every other day until the grass-like leaves dieback. This should occur around April. Once the leaves have died, move the container to a warm room that receives a lot of sunlight. Resume the every other day watering, and move outside as soon as your local frost-free date has passed.

Beyond flavoring, saffron has a reputation as an aphrodisiac. It is also used to treat coughs, gas, depression, hardening of the arteries, depression, and even dry skin. Some women use this spice to treat menstrual cramps, and premenstrual syndrome. Men, on the other hand, have used this herb in the treatment of premature ejaculation.

While all the uses noted above have been oral, some individuals apply saffron to the scalp in hopes of growing hair.

SAGE

Salvia officinalis

When you think of sage, you may reflect back upon Thanksgiving. This reminiscent smell of sage is what Claire picks up on while she is in Inverness (Outlander only, chapter 2). The background of the Latin name for sage can be translated to mean "to be saved." While there was no medical reason as to why individuals would combine sage and hyssop, form it into a pomander, and wear it around the next as a preventative measure against the plague, meaning of the Latin name may be why. The purser on board the Porpoise Mr. Overholt used sage and hyssop as a hopeful defense against the plague (Voyager, chapter 47).

Sage is noted to have some antiseptic properties that is why it can be used to treat cold sores, mouth sores, and swollen gums when directly applied. It can also be used to treat overproduction of sweat, and salvia. Other health issues that sage has been known to treat includes depression, digestive problems along with female issues such as painful cramps during menstruation. Some women also use sage to correct milk flow during nursing. Two unique uses for sage come into play in the treatment for asthma and Alzheimer. When sage is burned and the smoke is inhaled, some people who suffer from asthma have found relief. On the other hand, some evidence is available that says consuming sage can help balance the chemicals in the brain, which some feel is what causes the symptoms of the Alzheimer disease.

Sage is a perennial herb that is considered to be a hardy sub-shrub in USDA Plant Hardiness Zones 5 through 9. You can propagate this plant from seed, division and/or cuttings. While your sage plant can last forever, as the plant ages it becomes woodier. The best solution to this is to plan on replacing your sage every few years.

When it comes to propagating from seed, it is best to use this year's seed. Older sage seed typically has a poor germinate rate. To start your seeds indoors starts off with counting back eight weeks from your local frost-free date. Once you have that date, plan on cleaning and sterilizing your container(s). When it comes time to plant your seed, fill your container(s) with a moistened, well-draining potting soil. Next, sprinkle the seed on the soil surface. Barely cover the seed with soil. Mist with water, and place in a warm, sunny location. Keep the soil evenly moist. Be patient at this point, sage seeds can take up to 21 days to germinate.

Once the seeds have germinated and the seedlings are large enough to handle, transplant into individual pots. Place on a sunny windowsill.

If you would prefer to directly seed outdoors, prepare a garden space that receives full sun and is well-draining. Plant your seed as described above but put them out two weeks prior to your local frost-free date.

After your seeds have germinated, thin them out so that there is 24 to 30 inches between each plant.

Division is the next type of propagation for sage, and should be done in the spring. This process is simple. It only requires you to dig up the mother plant. Once you have it out of the ground, cut the root ball into several sections. Replant the mother plant. When it comes to planting the divisions, make sure the hole is the same depth as the root mass and twice the width.

After you have the hole dug, and tested the size, fill in around your sage division. Repeat the process making sure that you are properly spacing the divisions. Water in, and add more soil if needed. Monitor the soil moisture until the sage division has become established.

When it comes to propagating by cuttings, starts off with choosing the right material. You want young growth harvested in July through late summer. If you have no sage in your garden space, you can get cuttings from fresh herbs sold in the produce section at your local grocery store. How do you tell a young shoot? You are looking for one that looks succulent and non-woody. Once you have your eye on new growth, take a three to four-inch cutting. Remove all the leaves from the bottom up except three sets on the top. Prior to you taking your first cutting, you could have prepared pots for your cuttings, but sage is one of those herbs that roots well in water. In doing so, you can either root in the soil or place your cuttings in a glass of water. Change water daily to keep bacterial growth down. In about two weeks, you will see roots forming on the cuttings. Once that happens, pot them up into individual containers. This will be for a short time. The goal is to give the cutting a chance to take hold. Continue to monitor soil moisture. After you feel resistance when you gently pull on the cutting, you can plant your sage plant(s) in the garden.

SARACEN'S CONSOUND

Senecio saracenicus

Saracen's Consound belongs to a genus that includes over 1000 species. Some of these plants are succulents, while others are groundsels or ragworts. In this case, the Saracen's Consound is the broadleaf ragwort. But a common thread between all 1000 species is the fact that most are poisonous to animals. Another factor with it comes to this genus is the fact that groundsels and ragworts are noxious weeds. In doing so, growing directions will not be given.

The healing properties of this plant can be found in both the common and scientific name. As the story goes, Saracen used this herb to heal wounds. While it is not noted how in the research, Culpeper talks about collecting leaves and drying them for three days. After that, the leaves are taken down, cut into small pieces and put into a still that contains two gallons of molasses spirits (rum). Let this mixture stand for two days. Next, distill off one-and-a-half gallons of this mixture. Add one gallon of spring water along with half-a-pound of sugar to the distilled mixture. Allow it to sit for four days. After this, filter it. Once that is done, it is ready to use. You can also boil it with wine.

In the story, Master Raymond gives Claire this herb to treat Mary Hawkins private wounds after the rape. As he states, "good for soothing irritated skin, minor lacerations, and sores of the privy parts," (Dragonfly in Amber, chapter 20) so does Culpeper.

It was also noted to treat issues associated with the liver, and gallbladder..

SAXIFRAGE

Saxifraga or Pimpinella

In the Outlander book series and STARZ show, saxifrage is mentioned in a generic way. There are over 480 species of *Saxifrage* and more are being created every year. Whereas knowing where this plant was given to Claire may clear the picture up, the fact that this genus can be found worldwide complicates the issue.

Another issue comes about when one of the common names for *Pimpinella saxifrage* is saxifrage or burnet saxifrage. Since this plant is noted to grow in Europe, this is one that will be discussed.

This plant belongs to the same family as the wild carrot. It thrives in USDA Plant Hardiness Zones 4 through 8. Burnet saxifrage is not picky with the soil type, but it does require a soil that is well-draining and a little on the dry side. When it comes to the sunlight requirement, consider planting it in light shade to full sun. A great location that would meet this need would be along the edge of a woodland or hedgerow.

There does not exist much information on growing this plant. In just, it is better to let the plant reseed itself in the garden space. But what do you do if you do not have this plant? Well, this plant is often sold as an ornamental plant in many garden nurseries--but be careful. This plant is also classified as an invasive and can quickly take over grass-and-woodlands. The reason for this is the fact that this plant is prolific in seed production.

While Claire was pregnant, she had premature bleeding. Mother Hildegarde sent Claire a package of herbs that contained saxifrage, raspberry leaves and another ingredient, which she hoped would stop the bleeding (Dragonfly in Amber, chapter 23). It is not noted how Claire was to use this package of herbs but burnet saxifrage can be steeped in a bath. Once the steeping is complete, an individual can soak in this water to aid in the healing of wounds along with varicose veins. In combination with the other ingredients, this mixture could have been applied directly to the private parts to treat soreness.

Other aliments this plant is noted to treat include urinary tract infections, kidney stones, and problems with digestion. Presently, burnet saxifrage is being looked at as possible treatment for upper respiratory tract infections.

SELF HEAL

Prunella vulgaris

This herb belongs in the mint family since it has the characteristic square stem. Having said that, this plant does not have an aroma but it does have the spreading habit of mint. Self heal is hardy in USDA Plant Hardiness Zones 4 through 9. When it comes to growing this herb, you can either propagate from seed or purchase a plant. Sowing the seed should be done a week or two prior to your local frost-free date so that the seeds do get a little cold treatment. While you can start your seed indoor one to two months prior to your frost-free date, why would you when the planting process is so easy? Just prepare a garden spot that is in a sunny to partially shady area with well-draining soil. The process is simple. Just sprinkle the seed on the soil surface and mist with water. In a few days, you will see little sprouts of green appear on the soil surface. Now, you have self heal.

Since this herb can be invasive, you can either contain it in a bottomless pot or with a boarder buried deep in the soil. Another approach is to take a clay chimney flue that has been cut in half. This can then be placed in the garden and treated like a container. The weight of the clay will keep it up. The clay sides and depth of the container will keep it controlled.

If you do not want to go with either one of these containment ideas, simply let it go wild and use it as a ground cover or border. The purple flowers really pop when displayed growing untamed.

Do not fertilize this plant. To aid in the control, deadhead the plant often to reduce the number of seeds released into the environment.

If you do not want to plant seed, simply find a friend with this plant. Just as with mint, most gardeners with this herb will gracelessly share their crop through a division and/or cutting.

The history of self heal is very interesting. This plant's story starts off in ancient times along with a belief that physical characteristics of plant could explain their medical use (Doctrine of Signatures theory). In this case, the self heal has little barbs or thorns that go along the stem. Some individuals that followed the Doctrine of Signatures theory felt that this looked like a throat. In doing so, this herb was used in the treatment of mouth and throat inflammation.

Where the genus name *Prunella* comes from is another mystery. Some individuals feel that it refers to the purple flowers while other feel that the genus name is a misinterpretation of the German word Burnella. This German word means browns, which was a perfect description of what doctors were finding in the German soldiers during the 1547 through 1566. During this time period, an infection spread through the German military. The symptoms were sore throats and brown coated tongues.

Another nickname for this herb is carpenter's herb. This reflected the belief that this herb had the power to bring together and heal wounds both inside and out, hence the term self heal.

Chinese medicine views this herb as a "cooling" one. In doing, it is used to treat fevers. This may be due to the fact that recently it has been discovered to contain antioxidants, and chemicals that can be used as antibiotics. Since the consumption of this plant can increase circulation, some European herbalists are using this herb to treat mild headaches. Beyond these uses, self heal is known to treat irritable bowel syndrome, and liver disease. When applied to the skin, it can be used as a treatment for dry skin. Some women apply this herb to their private parts to take care of vaginal discharges and other female reproductive problems.

When Jamie and Claire first meet Hugh Munro, they are on a hilltop covered with self heal (Cross Stitch only, chapter 17).

SLIPPERY ELM

Ulmus rubra

Slippery Elm is indigenous to North America and Canada. It really loves growing in mountainous areas that have a moist environment and a dry soil. If this is a little confusing, think of the environment along the Appalachian Mountains where this tree can easily be found growing on the side of a mountain.

When it comes to growing this tree, you can find some potted or bare root trees for sale. While this will produce a mature tree faster, some studies have shown that locally grown plant material from a regional source is better. This type of plant material suffers less from plant disease and pests. In doing so, if you know where a Slippery Elm is located, consider harvesting the seeds yourself to grow your own tree. If you choose this approach, make sure you have permission of the landowner. Never take seeds or any other plant material from public lands.

Before you run out to the forest, make sure you are in the proper zone. Slippery Elm is native in USDA Plant Hardiness Zones 3 through 10. When mature, this tree can grow to 80 feet in height and an age of 200 hundred years. The heartwood of this tree is red, hence the common name Red Elm. Beyond these characteristics, this tree flowers before it leafs out in the early spring. While this is true with the American Elm, the bud and twigs of the Slippery Elm are hairy. On the other hand, the American Elm is not.

Now that you have found your Slippery Elm and the seeds have formed, gently shake the branches or handpick the seeds off the tree. Lay them out to dry for several days. If the "wings" are still left on the seed, leave them alone. Once the seeds have dried, you will need to soak them in water for 24 hours if you are going to plant immediately. On the other hand, if you are planning on planting later, place the seeds in a sealable bag filled with moistened soil. Place in the refrigerator for 60 to 90 days. When ready to plant, soak in water as described.

At this point, you have a few choices. You can plant your seeds in a flat, pot, peat pot or cold frame. In the urban environment, it really depends on the space you have and the number of seeds you are planting. To make transplanting easier, the directions will be given for peat pots. The reason for this choice is because when a tree seedling is transplanted, it is easy to damage the roots. To improve the success rate, peat pots are used that can be planted into and directly transplanted into the garden space.

Planting Slippery Elm seeds starts off with filling peat pots with an all-purpose potting soil medium that has been moistened. Next, place your seed on the soil surface and cover with 1/16 inch of soil. Put the planted peat pots in a sunny location. Check the soil daily. This is the trickiest part of this process. Slippery Elm likes a moist environment and a dry soil. To keep from getting the soil too moist, only water by placing the peat pots in a tray of water and allow the "peat" to become moist. This moisture will then, in turn, move into the soil.

Germination time period for the seeds varies. But as soon as the seedlings are large enough to be seen in the garden space, move them there. While some experts simply say to put the peat pot in the ground, I have learned a trick. First, let's in general talk about planting a tree. The hole must be the same depth of the container and twice the width. Once that hole has been dug, place the potted plant in the hole to test the size. Adjust as needed. Now you are ready to plant. These steps are the same for peat pots but there is one step more. Tear the top of the pot. If the peat pot is not completely covered with soil, the amount left above the soil will wick moisture away. While this tree does like it dry, it still needs moisture. In doing so, tearing the top down will prevent this from happening.

In the past, the inner bark of this tree was used to treat sore throats and coughs. It can also be turned into a balm that when applied to wounds and/or boils, speeds up healing. Other health ailments that Slippery Elm has been used to treat include; irritable bowel syndrome, colic, diarrhea, constipation, protect the stomach from ulcers, and urinary tract infections. When consumed, this plant is known to expel tapeworms.

It is noted that Claire has Slippery Elm in her medical bag that she carried with her while in Paris (Dragonfly in Amber, chapter 22). When Duncan Innes was suffering from constipation while on board the Artemis, Claire advised him that she would give him an enema if he did not have a bowel movement (Voyager, chapter 43).

Even though this tree is native to North America and nothing could be found as to this plant growing in Europe, I do believe that Claire got her supply from local apothecaries, such as Master Raymond's.

SOAPWORT

Saponaria officinalis

This perennial herb has a long history as a lathering cleaning agent for both clothes and skin. This "soap" comes from the sap of the plant. Soapwort's USDA Plant Hardiness Zones range from 2 through 8. In some situations, the hardiness of the plant makes it invasive but a great plant to naturalize areas. Claire sees this plant growing next to the millpond close to Lallybroch (Cross Stitch only, chapter 28). This location explains the growing requirements for this plant. Soapwort loves a moist, boggy soil that is located in the sun.

When it comes to propagating soapwort, you pick seed, division during the spring and fall, and cuttings. Propagating by seed will only be covered but do not forget to check the garden primer for directions on the other methods.

Starting your soapwort seed does not begin with planting the seed, but planning. Pull out your calendar and count back at least three months prior to your local frost-free date. The reason for such a long time is the fact that perennial soapwort seed can take up to three months to germinate. Once you have that date, you can schedule your seed treatment. Soapwort seed requires a cold treatment (stratification). To do this, dampen one paper towel, sprinkle your seed on the towel, and fold over. Place the treated paper towel in a sealable plastic bag. Place the sealed bag in your refrigerator for one week if you are going to start your seeds indoors. On the other hand, if you are going to directly seed into the garden, expose them to the cold of your refrigerator for two months.

At this point, when you are going to seed comes into play. Planting your seeds indoors after the chilling only requires one to remove the bag, remove the top layer of the paper towel, and place the paper towel with the seeds back into the bag. Put the bag on a sunny windowsill. Monitor the seeds and when you see them start to germinate, transplant them into individual peat pots. Place the seedlings on a sunny windowsill, and keep the soil moist. Two weeks prior to your local frost-free date, harden off the seedlings. Once this process has been completed, plant in the garden.

If you are going to directly seed into the garden, plant the cold treated seeds in the spring. Planting the seeds 16 to 18 inches apart will save time from thinning.

During the Middle Ages, Franciscan and Dominican monks viewed soapwort as a gift from the divine. This gift's purpose was to keep the monks clean. As the name applies, soapwort use included as soap but also as a treatment for the lungs, and skin. But the use depends on the type of soapwort. There is white and red soapwort. While both soapworts help with reducing the inflammation of the lungs, and coughing, the white soapwort treats chronic skin conditions. Red soapwort or bouncing bet offers relief from skin irritations such as poison ivy. It is also added to shampoos along with soaps. Surprisingly, the beer industry uses it due to its foam ability. In other words, it helps put a "head of foam" on your beer.

SORREL

Rumex acetosa

While sorrel is mentioned as an herb growing in the garden at Castle Leoch (Outlander, chapter 6), which is either *Rumex acetosa* (garden sorrel) or *Rumex acetosella (*common or sheep sorrel). Beyond these two varieties, sorrel is found in three other varieties. This includes French sorrel *(Rumex scutatus),* herb patience or spinach dock *(Rumex patient),* and spinach rhubarb (*Rumex abyssinicus).*

Apart from which variety you decide to grow, sorrel grows as a cool season perennial in USDA Plant Hardiness Zones 4 through 9. In other areas, this plant grows as an annual.

When it comes to growing sorrel, you are not limited to the garden and can easily grow this plant in a container. To get the most out of this cool season favorite, start your seeds four to six weeks prior to your local frost-free date. If you do not have the desire to start your seeds early, you can directly seed as early as three weeks from your frost-free date.

When you plant your seed, the process is easy and starts with adding aged manure or compost to the garden. Into this prepared garden space plant your sorrel seed ½ inch deep and two to three inches apart. Water the seeds in and keep the soil moist but not wet.

When the sorrel seedlings are six to eight weeks old, thin them out so that there is 12 to 18 inches between them. Planting sorrel in rows should only occur if you have room for a plant that requires 18 to 24 inches of space between rows.

In midsummer, add another layer of well seasoned manure or compost. This is also a great time to cut off any flowers that have appeared. Doing this simple task is a great way of keeping sorrel from becoming viewed as a weed in the garden.

Regardless of where you are going to display your sorrel, this plant loves full sun and a soil that is well-draining along with being rich in organic material.

Areas where sorrel grows as a perennial require division of the plant every two to three years.

Sorrel is a great companion to strawberries and other garden plants. The key though when using companion plantings and sorrel is to make sure the companion is not towering over the sorrel.

Interesting enough, sorrel gives food a certain flavor or sharpness verses making a whole salad of sorrel leaves. In doing so, keep this fact in mind and follow this simple planting formula. Each person in the household only need two to three sorrel plants for the season.

Sorrel when combined with other herbs is used as both a preventative and treatment for sinus and respiratory problems. Once taken with modern medications, this mixture treats bacterial infections. Other uses for sorrel include as a diuretic and part of an herbal cancer treatment.

SOW FENNEL

Peucedanum officinale

The sow or hog's fennel is one that is being seen more in the wild in North America. The USDA Plant Hardiness Zones for this biennial are 6a through 8b. While sow fennel is somewhat of a general term, there is the giant and sea hog's fennel. The general appearance is the same. Sow or hog's fennel reaches a mature height of three to four feet. It has a flower head covered in bright yellow flowers much like the dill. The difference though can be found when the root is cut and explains the origins of one of the nicknames, which is sulfurwort. When the roots of this plant are cut, the aroma of sulfur emits from the root.

Hog's fennel is a biennial/perennial that is monocarpic. What this term means is that the plant will continue to grow until it flowers. Once that happens the plant dies. When this plant does flower, the flower heads should be removed so that the seeds can be collected. Or, leave the seed heads. This will give the plant a chance to reseed itself naturally.

When it comes to the ideal location for your sow fennel, pick a soil that is moist but well-draining. While it does its best in a location that receives full sun, it can tolerate areas of partial shade.

The planting process is simple and begins with a broadcasting of the seed over the planned area. Next, water the seed in and do not allow the soil to dry out.

While there was no set time period by which the seeds will germinate, it is noted that the seeds germinate quickly.

When it comes to spacing, this depends on the type of sow fennel you have planted but the recommend spacing is between 9 and 24 inches.

It is noted that all parts of the plant are poisonous and even contact with the sap from the roots can cause photo-sensitivity and/or dermatitis in the area that was touched.

In the past, sow fennel was mixed in vinegar and rose water. This solution was rubbed in the nose as a treatment for headaches, and laziness. When the root was juiced and mixed with a little wine, it could be used as way of dealing with pain from ones ear or tooth.

Sow fennel's role in the story comes from a suggestion from Claire that preparing a willow bark tea with this herb may give Jamie some relief from his hangover headache (Dragonfly in Amber, chapter 6).

ST. JOHN'S WORT

Hypericum

The genus *Hypericum* contains over 300 varieties but the common St. John's Wort is known as *Hypericum perforatum.* This little perennial shrub is resilient in USDA Plant Hardiness Zones 4 through 8 while some sources extend it to zone 10. Due to this plant's spreading nature, this plant has become an invasive nuisance.

This herb is known as a treatment for depression and symptoms associated with this disease, which includes anxiety, trouble sleeping, and/or loss of appetite. But this herb is also used to treat other mental issues along with problems related to menstruation; which include premenstrual syndrome, and menopause. An oil of St. John's Wort can be taken orally to treat digestive issues. When this oil is applied to the skin, it aids in wound healing, inflammation, bug bites, and hemorrhoids. It has also been used to treat a little known skin disease by which the skin pigment disappears (Vitiligo).

This herb is mentioned several times in the Outlander book series and adaptation from STARZ. Its use as a wound treatment is brought forth when the leaves and/or flowers are ground up and soaked in vinegar (Outlander, chapter 6). The antiviral, antibacterial, and antioxidant nature of this herb fits its use as a disinfectant for wounds (Outlander, chapter 38) along with a treatment for wounds already infected (Dragonfly in Amber, chapter 12). The overall usefulness of this herb is why Claire included it in her medical kit that she carried on the voyage to the West Indies while looking for of Ian (Voyager, chapter 40).

While any of the varieties of *Hypericum* can be come invasive, they do look wonderful in containers, rock gardens, and as an edging. This plant is not picky about the soil but it is a good idea to mix in two inches of well seasoned compost or manure to the planned garden space. Mix this into the soil to a depth of eight inches.

Many sources state that St. John's Wort needs full sun, but there is a fine line of proper sunlight. Too much sun will burn the leaves while not enough sunlight will cause the plant to produce fewer blooms. The best solution is to make sure that your St. John's Wort receives morning sunlight and a little shade in the afternoon.

Propagating this herb can occur through rooting stem cuttings and/or seeds. You can also find a variety of *Hypericum* in garden nurseries. Most of these ornamental cultivators do not have the self-seeding problem, which in some areas makes this plant invasive or weedy.

Since the stem cutting requires a plant, this will be covered later in the pruning section.

When it comes to starting St. John's Wort seeds, you have a choice of indoors or out. The process for either is the same but the planting time is different.

If you are a forgetful gardener when it comes to your outside plants, then the indoor method would be best. You need to plan on planting your seed 10 to 12 weeks prior to your local frost-free date. On the other hand, if you do not have the space, planting your St. John's Wort seed is no problem after your local frost-free date.

Planting indoors starts off with the planned date. Once you have that, clean and sterilize a flat or pot. Next, fill the container with a well-draining all-purpose potting soil medium. Add water to the soil until you see moisture coming out the bottom of the container. Now, your container is ready to plant.

St. John's Wort seed requires light to germinate. What this means is you will simply sprinkle the seed on the soil surface. Mist the soil with water. Place your planted container in a warm and sunny location.

Continue to monitor the soil moisture making sure the potting medium never dries out. Once the seedlings are large enough to handle, transplant them into individual pots. A week prior to your local frost-free date, harden off the plants before planting in the garden.

Directly seeding into the garden space starts off with preparing the area. Remove any unwanted plant material and prepare the soil as noted earlier. After your local frost-free date has arrived, you can plant your seed outside. The process only requires one to sprinkle the seed on the prepared soil and gently water in. As before, keep the soil evenly moist.

Regardless of which technique you choose, your seeds will take 14 to 30 days to germinate.

To save seed, space them so that there is 12 to 18 inches between plants and in rows that are 36 inches apart.

Once the seedlings are large enough to handle, thin them out so that there is 24 to 36 inches between plants.

If planting a garden nursery specimen, prepare the garden space as described. Dig a hole that is twice the width and the same depth as the container. Test the hole by placing the potted plant inside. Adjust as needed. Once the hole is correct, remove the plant from the container; tease the roots by loosening the soil, and place your plant in the hole. Fill in with removed soil, water in, and add soil as needed. As noted, the spacing needs to be 24 to 36 inches.

Beyond watering your St. John's Wort until it gets established, you will need to prune it. There are several reasons for this but the two top are that pruning reduces self seeding and it keeps the plant healthy.

Pruning should begin in March. During this time, you will remove one-third of the plant. Once that is done, thin out some of the branches to allow light and air in. Also, cut away any dead plant material.

If your St. Johns Wort has not been producing many blooms, rejuvenate it by cutting it down to one to two inches above ground level. Believe it or not, the plant will come back from this cutting full of blooms.

When it comes to taking cutting from this plant, the key is to harvest new growth early in the spring. Make the cut at an angle with a sharp knife. Dip the cut end in root hormone. Using a pencil, make a hole in the planting medium and place your cutting in the hole. Seal the soil around the hole. Repeat as needed. Gently water the soil and place your planted cutting in a shady location. Monitor soil moisture. In several weeks, you should be able to gently tug on these cuttings to feel resistance. At this point, transplant into pots or garden.

STONEROOT

Collinsonia canadensis

Stoneroot is one of those plants whose common name tells a story. The true meaning of this common name may not be known, but there are two reasons why the term stoneroot describes this perennial plant perfectly. The first reason is that the rhizome of this plant is very hard like a stone. The second reason comes from the tea that was made by mountaineers for the treatment of kidney stones.

Beyond using stoneroot to treat kidney stones, this herb has also been used as a treatment for headaches, indigestion, and water retention. In the story, Claire would be found pounding the herb's root so that she could use it in her surgery while at Leoch (Outlander only, chapter 24)

The USDA Plant Hardiness Zones are 4 through 8. While growing this herb is not difficult, you will want to start off with seed. To get the best results, make sure to plant the seed as soon as it is ripe in the fall. If that is not possible, you can still plant it in the spring but expect the seeds to take longer to germinate.

When it comes to planting the seeds, do not directly seed into the garden space. The best approach is to plant them in a cold frame by simply sprinkling the seed on top of the soil. In eight to ten weeks, the seeds will germinate and should remain in the cold frame until they are large enough to handle without harm.

Once they can be safely removed from the cold frame, place in individual containers. Move the pots to a shady location and keep the soil moist. The plants will remain here until they are two years old. After that, they can be moved to an area in the garden that is moist and is covered with dappled shade.

Once the seedlings are three years old, they can be divided are replanted into separate clumps.

If you are looking for some ideas on how to use stoneroot in your garden, consider planting it in along the edge of a woodland landscape or bog garden. Another idea is to nestle it among trees with shallow roots. Regardless of where you plant your stoneroot, remember that it has a large roots and a mature height of four feet so plan accordingly. Also, some individuals are bothered by the aroma of the foliage, which is described as a strong lemony scent. In doing so, planting it in a location where the leaves will not be bruised or brushed often may be a good idea.

STORKSBILL

Erodium spp.

Through research there are two species of *Erodium* that go by storksbill. This includes the *Erodium reichardii* and *Erodium cicutarium.* Both of these have the common name storksbill. Regardless of the Latin name, both of these plants can be an annual, semi-annual or a hardy perennial. The growth cycle depends on where you live.

The natural habitat of the storksbill is western Asia and the Mediterranean. Due to this fact, this plant is hardy in USDA Plant Hardiness Zones 7 through 10.

The genus *Erodium* is one that can take a lot of abuse. In doing so, many people grow this plant in high traffic areas since it can survive when walked on. Its low growth habit also makes it a favorite for rock gardens.

You may wonder why there is confusion with the plant. The reason for this is the fact that the term stork's bill actually describes the seed. The seed of the *Erodium* has a hook or "beak-like" structure on it, hence the generic name.

When it comes to propagating your storksbill, it is better to directly seed into the garden in the fall. The location of this space needs to be in full sun if you want to take advantage of this plant prolific blooming nature but it can tolerate and area that receives some shade.

Soil conditions are another requirement that this plant finds flexibility in. It thrives in rocky soil that is well-draining and slightly alkaline.

When it comes to planting your storksbill seeds, just sprinkle on the prepared soil surface, and cover with 1/8 inch of soil. Water the seeds in to settle them down on top of the soil. Depending on the environment, you could see signs of seed germination anytime between planting and spring.

Once your seedlings have several leaves, thin them out so that there is six to eight inches between the plants.

Water more often when the plant is blooming, which can occur from April to October. Once the plant goes dormant, stop watering. Add a three-inch layer of mulch in the fall.

Erodium can also be propagated through division, and basal stem cuttings in the spring.

Storksbill is not started indoors to get a jump on the season but some individuals grow this plant as a houseplant.

In the storyline (Outlander only, chapter 16), Claire notes that storksbill is a plant that can be used to treat headaches. Again, the name confusion played in the research. WebMD, listed Herb Robert with the common name storksbill. In doing so, I have included the uses of Herb Robert in with the research done on storksbill.

While research did not show that this plant is used directly to treat headaches, Native Americans did use it to reduce bleeding after giving birth. Women would also consume it to increase milk production. The only evidence that could be found for pain relief comes from the chewing of the leaves to reduce the pain from a sore mouth and/or throat. But it was noted that a large amount needs to be consumed before any results can be felt.

Another use for storksbill comes from its aroma. The smell of this plant can only be described as terrible. Taking advantage of this natural insect repelling habit, medieval people would use it to keep pest away from their home, their body and their livestock. This latter occurred when the plant would be mixed into the bedding for the animal.

TANSY

Tanacetum vulgare

This perennial, herbaceous herb is one that is easily found growing wild in the Highlands of Scotland (Outlander only, chapter 17). Tansy also reappears as a plant that Claire picks on a walk to the mill at Lallybroch with Jamie (Outlander, chapter 28). While this plant has been used as a flavoring and medicine, Claire picked this herb because of its beauty. The leaves resemble that of fern. The bright yellow flowers are supported on long stems, which can reach three feet in height. Tansy flowers have a unique shape that is indicated by one of its common names. The common name Golden Buttons explains the flat topped, button shaped bloom that tops the flower stalks.

Beyond the beauty of the flowers, many gardeners grow tansy for its camphor aroma. This aroma is unpleasant to garden pests. In doing so, this herb is planted to keep garden pests at bay without chemicals.

Tansy is a hardy perennial in USDA Plant Hardiness Zones 4 through 8. In some areas, this herb is labeled weedy due to the fact that it spread by seed and rhizomes.

When it comes to propagating this herb, the techniques are by seed and division. The propagation technique that will be covered is through seed but check the garden primer section for directions on dividing the plant.

Starting tansy from seed is simple but you will need to decide which approach you want to take. Some individuals have found that direct seeding the seeds in the garden spare is fine. Others believe it is better to start the seeds indoors and then transplant after the local frost-free date. The technique you choose is up to you.

Regardless of the environment you pick to start your seed, it is important to only cover them with ¼ inch of soil and keep the planting medium moist. In 7 to 10 days, you should see little green dots of growth. If you directly seeded, thin them out so that there is six inches between seedlings.

On the other hand, if you started your seeds indoors, transplant them into individual pots once they have several sets of leaves.

Two weeks prior to your local frost-free date, harden the seedlings off. Pick a sunny to partially shady location that has a well-draining soil. There is no reason to worry if the soil is poor in fertility. Tansy prefers soils that are average or below in fertility.

Once planted, water tansy when the soil is dry until established. After that, tansy only requires watering when a drought is long term.

While tansy can be divided in the spring and/or fall, it is better to divide in the early spring. Choosing to divide tansy in the spring will give your plant the time to reestablish itself in the garden before winter.

THYME

Thymus vulgaris

While it is not noted as to whether wild thyme or what is viewed today as culinary thyme, is what Claire requests Mrs. Fitz to fetch for her to treat Jamie's wound while at Castle Leoch (Cross Stitch only, chapter 4). The culinary version appears to have some antibacterial and antifungal properties. There was no clear evidence of this herb being used directly on wounds but it is rubbed on the skin to treat hoarseness, sore mouth, and swollen tonsils.

Culinary thyme is a perennial shrub that grows easily in USDA Plant Hardiness Zones 5 through 9. When it comes to growing thyme, you have three choices. One is to purchase plants that are relatively available at garden stores. Two is to purchase seed and three, purchasing "cutting" from your local grocery store. While the grocery store variety will grow, you will not know which one of the over fifty varieties you have bought.

The easiest way of growing your thyme is through purchased plants. The reason for this is the fact that thyme has an uneven germination rate, but you can still find success in seed propagation.

To start your thyme seeds, begin with pulling out your calendar and counting back 6 to 10 weeks before your local frost-free date. This is the date by which you should begin planting your thyme seed. Prior to this date, prepare your pot or flat by cleaning and sterilizing it.

Next, fill the container with an all-purpose potting. Since the thyme seeds are small, mist the soil until you see moisture come out the bottom of the container. Once the soil is evenly moist, sprinkle the seeds on the soil surface and cover with 1/8 inch of soil. Place the container on a sunny windowsill and monitor soil moisture. Only water when the soil feels dry.

In 8 to 20 days, you will begin to see thyme seedling beginning to appear. One to two weeks prior to your local frost-free date, harden off your seedlings and move to the garden or transplant into containers. For proper growth, thyme planted in the garden needs to be spaced 18 to 24 inches apart.

As mentioned before, you can get a start of thyme from the produce section of your local grocery store, but there a few things you need to do to get the "cutting" to grow.

First, you need to select the healthiest "cutting" you can find. Next, make a fresh, angled cut on the herbal stem. Remove any leaves 2 inches up the stem. Dip the stem in a rooting hormone and place in a container filled with moistened planting medium. Repeat until you have processed all the "cut" thyme. Place your prepared cuts in a clear, plastic bag and tie off the top. Put your container filled with cutting in a location by which it receives indirect sunlight.

While you have made a mini-greenhouse that conserves moisture, it is still a good idea to check the soil. Add water only when the soil feels dry.

In eight weeks, your cutting should be forming roots. At this point, put them in individual pots.

As with seedlings, you will need to harden the rooted cuttings off. When ready to move to the garden, make sure to plant your time in a location that is well-draining and exposed to full sun or partial shade.

TURMERIC

Curcumae longae

If you live in a warm, tropical environment, you will have no problem growing turmeric outdoors. Those who live in the USDA Plant Hardiness Zones 7b through 10b will also find success growing this herbaceous plant outside. It will thrive during the spring and summer while dying back in the fall. But, if you not live in a tropical paradise, do not worry. Turmeric can easily be grown in a container.

Both planting techniques will be described but they start off with acquiring your turmeric root. The easiest way to get your root is to stop by a grocery store. Today, many grocery stores carry the fresh root. The key though is to pick the healthiest roots you can find and purchase more than one. While you are looking through the bin of turmeric root, you may notice some differences on the surface of each root. Little knobs will appear where buds will form while the smoother area is the location of the roots. Knowing this is very important when it comes time to planting the root.

To plant your turmeric in a container, begins with creating a little greenhouse which will mimic the tropics. The process is simple and begins with cleaning and sterilizing a flat or shallow pot. Once that is done, mix up your planting medium by combining one part sand to one part well-seasoned compost. Next, moisten this mixture and place in the prepared container.

Now that your container is ready to plant, take a look at your turmeric roots. If you have some that are branched, cut off the branches. This will give you more turmeric to plant or cook with. Next, take a look at the first root you plant to plant and place in the container so that the knobs or buds are up and the roots are down. Create a shallow trench in the soil, place your root in the trench and just cover the root. Repeat with all the roots.

Place your flat or container in a clear, sealable plastic bag. Close the bag and place in a warm location away from any sun exposure. A great location is on top of your refrigerator, which will provide bottom heat.

In about a week to a month, you should see the buds begin to form and open. Once that has happened, remove the container from the plastic bag and place the container in a warm room. Avoid direct sunlight; this will burn the young leaves of your plant. Instead, place on a hard surface that is exposed to indirect sunlight.

Check soil moisture and do not allow the planting medium to dry out. Once the turmeric root has developed several roots and the vegetation is two inches tall, transplant your root to a six-inch container that has been filled with a DIY planting medium of one part well-seasoned compost to one part potting soil. Plant the growing roots shallowly as you did in the beginning and water in until you see moisture come out the bottom of the container.

Position your newly planted root in a warm location away from drafts and bright sunlight. Monitor soil moisture and water as needed. As fall and winter approach, expose your planted turmeric root to more sunlight. Reduce the exposure when spring and summer arrive.

Feed your planted turmeric root with a balanced fertilizer, such as a 10-10-10 once a week during the spring and summer months. Also, mist with water or place on a humidity tray your turmeric plant during the times when your air-conditioning or heat is on.

While growing turmeric root indoors can occur anytime, the root itself should only be planted outdoors in the fall. You can directly plant into the prepared garden space. Or to get a jump on the season, start indoors as described previously.

Regardless if you decide to grow your turmeric as an indoor plant or in your garden space, give it room. For proper growth, each plant will need to be spaced 12 to 16 inches apart.

When it comes to harvesting, it will take seven to nine months from the time you planted your sprouted turmeric root to when the root is large enough to be dug up.

Davie Beaton used turmeric in a treatment for jaundice (Outlander, chapter7). While no direct evidence could be found that turmeric in any treatment for jaundice, it is noted that this herb has seen some promise in the treatment of stomach issues such as stomach ulcers, and upset stomach. In preliminary studies, the chemical found in turmeric, curcumin, has been found to reduce inflammation brought on by osteoarthritis and rheumatoid arthritis.

VALERIAN

Valeriana officinalis

This perennial herb has a long history that spans the centuries. It has been used as a treatment for anxiety and sleeping disorders. In the 16th century, the valerian flowers were picked and the oils were harvested for the perfume industry. In Greece, this herb was used to treat aliments of the liver, urinary tract, and digestive system. During WWI and WWII, valerian use resurfaced as a treatment for battle related stress.

Valerian use was also a component of a love spell. It was believed that this herb would keep lovers from fighting. This belief carried over to weddings with the groom stashing away little packets of valerian in their wedding clothes. The theory behind this approach was that the aroma would keep evil elves away from the wedding bed.

The use of this herb as a stress and anxiety reducer is why Claire chose to give Jamie dried valerian while they were at the Abbey of Ste. Anne de Beaupre. She also picked this herb for its belief in chasing away evil spirits since she was trying to exorcise his demons (Outlander, chapter 39).

Another use that is noted in the Outlander series is as a form of birth control that some French midwives used. Claire had mentioned this to Marsali. It was noted by Claire that the combination of valerian and bayberry was dangerous and not very reliable (Voyager, chapter 48). No research could be found that supported this historical use.

The root of the valerian historically was dried and used as a spice in stews and salads.

Common valerian, which is the standard variety, can be grown from seed or division in USDA Plant Hardiness Zones 4a through 9b. If you are not an experienced gardener, the division approach is your best bet and your fellow gardener's best approach since this plant can be invasive.

When it comes to growing valerian from seed, you have two choices. It can be seeded directly into the garden soil or you can get a jump on the season by starting your seeds indoors 4 weeks prior to your local frost-free date. Regardless of when you choose to plant your seed, you will need to make sure that you have the best location picked out. Valerian loves 6 to 8 hours of full sun but can tolerate some shade. The soil needs to be well-draining.

As you prepare to plant your valerian seed, you will notice how small the seed is. In doing so, you simply need to sprinkle the seed on top of the prepared garden space or two-inch container filled with all-purpose potting soil. Top the seeds with ¼ inch of potting soil and place on a sunny windowsill. Seeds will germinate in 7 t o14 days.

Continue to monitor soil moisture and water as needed. Since this plant is a fast grower, you will probably need to move it to a six-inch deep container before it is time to plant in the garden.

When you are ready to plant your valerian in the garden space, make sure to give it some room. Valerian requires 24 to 36 inches between each plant. Once you have planted this herb in the garden space, top the soil with well-seasoned compost and a thick layer of mulch. Continue to monitor the soil moisture since this is a plant that does not tolerate dry conditions very well.

A unique aspect of this herb may be surprising. Believe it or not, cats love this herb. They love to roll and sleep in it. This was such a common occurrence that ancient herbalists used the activity of cats around and on valerian as a gauge to measure the potency of the herb.

VANILLA

Vanilla planifola

Believe it or not, *Vanilla planifola* belongs to the orchid family. The vanilla orchid has over 100 species and is a vine that can reach over 300 feet in height. When it comes to growing the vanilla orchid, there are two important factors. One, creating the proper environment and two, hand pollinating. Due to the particular environmental requirements, some find growing it in a greenhouse is easier but if you do not have a glass house, do not worry. The vanilla orchid can be grown right in your home.

The first step of this process is to purchase your vanilla orchid. While you can grow this plant from seed, it will take a lot longer to produce the vanilla pod, which requires plants to be 3 to 5 years of age.

Once your plant has arrived, you will need to transplant it into a larger container, preferably an orchid pot. If you do not have an orchid container, you can still use a traditional pot.

After the container has been cleaned, and sterilized, fill it up the container one-third with an orchid soil or fir bark and terrestrial planting medium. Next, take a sharp knife and wipe it down with rubbing alcohol. Once that is done, gently squeeze the sides of the pot that your vanilla orchid is in to release the plant. Tip it upside down and squeeze again until the plant falls into your hands. If the pot is plastic, you can also slit the sides of the container to remove the plant.

After the plant has been removed from the pot, cut off one-third of the root mass from the bottom with the sterilized knife. Loosen the roots and place in the new container. Fill in with the planting medium mentioned previously. Gently tap the planted container on a hard surface to settle the soil. Since the vanilla orchid is a vine, place a tall stake into the container.

Move your vanilla orchid to a room that receives medium sunlight to partial shade and is kept around 86 degrees Fahrenheit during the day and 50 degrees Fahrenheit at night. To increase the humidity around the plant, put the container on a humidity tray or display your vanilla orchid in the bathroom. This latter location normally meets the humidity and temperature requirement but the sunlight may be an issue. Regardless, to add a fan to the room by which your vanilla orchid is displayed.

When it comes to watering your vanilla orchid, this can be a little challenging. You want to keep the soil evenly moist but at the same time you want to allow the top two inches to dry out between watering. To encourage blooming, you will need to feed your orchid a half-strength dilution of orchid fertilizer every two weeks during the spring and summer months.

If you are lucky, your vanilla orchid will bloom but it will need a little help to produce vanilla. This little encouragement comes from hand pollination. Below is just a general description on how to do this task. To increase your chances of success, you will need to perform this several times during the blooming season.

The process of hand pollination starts off with taking a toothpick and collecting pollen from the anther. Once the pollen is on the tip of the toothpick, move it over to the stigma, which is covered with a hood. Gently lift up the shield and place the pollen alongside the column. Put the shield back over the stigma. If pollination has occurred, your vanilla pod will begin to form but will take eight to nine months to mature.

Due to vanilla's culinary delight, Claire used this and other herbs to bribe the cook on the Artemis, Mr. Murphy (Voyager, chapter 41).

When it comes to the uses for vanilla beyond baking, they run a unique path. Smelling vanilla extract has been found to have a calming effect. Ancient people believed that vanilla was an aphrodisiac. Its antibacterial nature has made it a component of acne creams and anti-aging products. Another unique use of this herb comes from the vanilliods it contains. Similar substances can be found in chili peppers as capsaicin, and eugenols found in cinnamon. All of these affect the nervous system to relive pain. Finally, the simple vanilla bean also contains anti-inflammatory substances along with antioxidants.

WOOD SORREL

Oxalis spp.

Since the particular species is not noted in the story, and there are over 300 different species of *Oxalis,* general information will be provided for the plant.

Wood sorrel is considered a hardy perennial plant in USDA Plant Hardiness Zones 5 to 11. It is typically grown indoors as a houseplant during St. Patrick's Day but is just as easy to grow outside.

This plant can be started by seed but the simplest way is through the "bulb" or rhizome that it produces. These are easily found in seed catalogues. While you are waiting for your rhizomes to come in, you can begin to select and prepare the garden space.

The first matter at hand is the proper location and time of planting. Wood sorrel requires a sunny location but can tolerate partial shade. It also needs a well-draining soil. To aid in the drainage and fertility of the soil, mix in 3 to 6 inches of well-seasoned compost and/or manure. If the soil is a little on the dry side, consider adding some peat moss to the mix but do this with a light hand. Soil that is too wet will cause the rhizomes to rot.

Mix your soil additions down 10 to 12 inches. Once that is done, plan out your design so that you have 6 inches between each planting. Next dig a half to one-inch deep hole and plant three to four wood sorrel rhizomes in the hole. Fill in the hole with the removed soil and continue planting. After all the rhizomes have been planted, water in the garden space.

Monitor soil moisture and water when the soil becomes dry. Once you see little leaves begin to appear from the ground, feed your wood sorrel a balanced, water- soluble fertilizer such as a 15-15-15 once a week.

When you see your wood sorrel plants begin to decline, stop watering and fertilizing. Do not be alarmed though when this happens. This dieback is a natural process of the wood sorrel and in some species happens several times over the growing season.

Please note that *Oxalis spp.* in some areas is considered an invasive species. Check with your local extension agent before planting.

Wood sorrel should not be confused with sorrel. The uses of wood sorrel include as a source of Vitamin C, and to treat liver and/or digestive problems.

In the storyline, Claire and Geillis Duncan, initially met while Claire was looking for wood sorrel (Cross Stitch only, chapter 9).

WORMWOOD

Artemisia absinthium

Wormwood has a unique history and this historical narration starts off with the Latin name (*Artemisia absinthium).* The name *Artemisia* is derived from the name of a Greek goddess Artemis. This goddess was the one that watched over women during childbirth. This herb was also used to bring on periods. The Ancient Egyptians also used this herb to treat intestinal worms, which included round worms, and threadworms. Later on, wormwood's ability to repel insects was noted and used. When planted as a companion plant in the garden, wormwood repels cabbageworm butterflies, slugs, aphids, and black flea flies. When the leaves of this perennial herb are dried and placed in sachets, the aroma of this herb keeps moths at bay.

While the repelling nature of this herb may be a little secret, a well-known use of this herb is for flavoring for alcohol beverages such as Vermouth and Absinthe. Due to the toxic nature of the thujone, which is produced by the wormwood herb, Absinthe is banned in many countries.

Beyond using this herb for intestinal problems, it can also be applied to skin to treat wounds, and even insect bites. Many artists valued wormwood for its ability to create hallucination. In the storyline (Outlander, chapter 7), wormwood is mentioned as an herb present at Davie Beaton's surgery while at Castle Leoch.

Wormwood belongs to a large genius of plants that include members such as tarragon, and sagebrush. While this herb can be found growing wild along the roadsides in Europe, it also grows well in USDA Plant Hardiness Zones 3 through 9.

When it comes to propagating this herb, you have three choices. If you know someone with this herb, consider asking them if you can take some semi-hardwood cuttings in the late summer to early fall. Another choice is to acquire a root cutting in the autumn. If neither one of these propagation methods are possible, you can grow wormwood from seed.

Propagating wormwood from seed starts off with a little homework in the autumn. The first thing you will need to do is to gather a garden flat. Once you have that item, you will need to prepare a growing location for your seeds. Wormwood seeds should not be started indoors and to keep the soil from freezing, you will need to dig a hole by which your flat fits into. Once that is done, you will need to wash and sterilize your flat and fill with an all-purpose potting soil.

Once that is done, water the soil in until you see moisture coming out of the bottom of the flat. Next, sprinkle the seeds on top of the soil surface and cover with a clear pane of glass. The reason for the clear glass is the fact that wormwood seeds require sunlight to germinate.

After you have planted your flat, place it in the hole that you have dug. Germination of wormwood seed can take between two and nine weeks with an optimum temperature of 55 to 65 degrees Fahrenheit.

Once you begin to see little dots indicating seed germination, remove the glass pane and monitor the soil moisture. Protect from frost anytime temperatures drop below 55 degrees Fahrenheit.

Plant your wormwood seedlings in the garden space after your local frost-free date. When planning this process, choose a location wisely. Wormwood's mature size is two to three feet in height and requires at least 12 inches to 24 inches between plants. In doing so, this plant needs space, but it also requires a well-draining soil and a sunny to partially shady location.

Now that you have the ideal location selected, your local frost-free date has passed, and your wormwood seedlings have at least two sets of leaves, you are ready to plant them in the garden.

During the summer months, water as needed and feed a balanced fertilizer such as a 10-10-10. Do not feed the fertilizer at full strength instead dilute it to 1/5 the strength. Apply once a month. Another approach is to add 2 inches of well-seasoned compost to the soil surface in place of the fertilizer.

To keep wormwood looking its best and to prevent the spreading of the plant, deadhead the flowers throughout the summer. Rake up any wormwood debris on the ground. This simple task will reduce the chances of developing fungal problems. Prune back the plant in midsummer to half its height to encourage bushy growth.

During the autumn, cut the plant back to the point that only two inches remain above the soil line. Top the soil with three to four inches of mulch in the winter to protect the root ball. Divide the plant every three to four years. But do not simply dig the plant up, divide and replant. The best approach is to divide the outer boundary of the plant while throwing away the center, which normally has become woody. Do not decompose any wormwood plant material.

YARROW

Achillea millefoliu

Believe it or not, the scientific name for yarrow gives a hint to its history. The genus name *Achillea* comes from the story that Achilles used yarrow to try to stop the bleeding of his soldiers. The common name for this plant is also an indication of its history and includes Knight Milfoil, and Soldier's Wound Wort. It was also referred to as Nosebleed, which came from the habit of rolling the leaves of this plant and placing it up the nose to stop the bleeding.

In Europe, this herb was also used to treat digestive problems. While they did not understand why this herb worked, it has been found that yarrow contains flavonoids, which increases saliva and stomach acid. Other uses for yarrow include treating colds, and breaking or reducing fevers. This fever-reducing property that yarrow has is why Claire used it to treat a fever while she was at the Abbey de Beaupre (Cross Stitch, chapter 39)

It is also known to keep pests at bay, which was observed by Mrs. FitzGibbons (Outlander, chapter 6). Yarrow is also an excellent anti-microbial that can be used as a disinfectant (Outlander, chapter 38).

When it comes to growing this perennial, you have two choices. You can propagate yarrow from seed or division. Starting your yarrow seed indoors can be a challenge but it is doable. To begin the process, one must first pull out your calendar and count back six to eight weeks from your local frost-free date. Once you have that date, you are ready to start planting your seed.

After you have filled your container with an all-purpose potting soil, gently sprinkle the seeds on top. Cover with a slightly layer of soil that should not be any deeper than ¼ inch. Place the container on a sunny windowsill.

In 14 to 21 days, you should see evidence that your seeds have germinated. Continue to monitor the soil's moisture and water accordingly.

When it comes to yarrow's growing requirements, it does need at least six to eight hours of full sun and a well-drained soil. It is hardy in USDA Plant Hardiness Zones 3 through 9.

Once the location has been picked, plant your yarrow so that it has room to grow, which means each two feet between plants. After all the plants have been placed in the ground, top the soil with well-seasoned compost and two inches of mulch.

While you may be familiar with the yellow flowers and gray-green foliage of the common garden yarrow, there are other varieties. Coastal is one type that can be found growing naturally on the coast of Oregon and California. This type has the largest flower head and the strongest aroma. Colorado mix has huge flower heads but not as large as the Coastal. The flowers come in red, pink, yellow, and apricot. Cloth of Gold has flower heads that are the brightest yellow color of all the yarrows. Parker's variety looks much like the wild type but the flower heads are smaller.

YAWROOT

Stillingia sylvatica

This perennial herb is also known as Queen's Root, Silverleaf, Queen's Delight, and Sapium Sylvaticum Yaw Root. It is commonly found in the United States along with Africa, and in Mediterranean. This plant can grow up to four feet in height and produces yellow green "flowers" without petals that are supported on spikes. There are a vast number of uses for this plant, which includes--as a laxative, blood cleaner, and as a substance that encourages vomiting.

As noted in the Outlander series, yawroot is used to treat skin ailments. This common use can be found when Claire made an ointment from yawroot to treat eczema and a burn salve (Outlander, chapter 7).

There is not much known about this plant, but what can be gathered is the fact that it can be found in sunny to partially shady areas. These areas also contain sandy soil, which makes it a wonderful choice for drought resistance landscaping or xeriscaping.

Garden History At Versailles

In the Outlander book series and STARZ show, Jamie and Claire are invited to Versailles. While not much time is spent filming the inside of Versailles, different areas of the gardens are used as a backdrop for the storyline. To really appreciate the gardens, we must understand their conception.

The basic history of European garden design starts off with the Roman Empire. During this time period, the gardens were formal with neatly trimmed hedges. These hedges created little niches by which garden art would be displayed. For convenience, small kitchen gardens were placed near the palace and consisted of fruits and vegetables, which were native to the area.

The Medieval time period saw the planting of not only kitchen gardens but also herbs gardens. Monasteries began to create green space for contemplation of religion. To keep the green space neat and tidy, walkways were designed around the space. Adding to the calming environment, many monasteries green spaces had a center focal point, which was a well or fountain.

Landscape design for castles was a little different compared to the monasteries. At this point in time, small courtyard gardens were in fashion. Just as in the monastery, paths were created that meandered around raised beds full of blooming flowers. Another feature of the medieval landscape design was that of raised mounds of turf that formed seating areas. These areas where built high enough so that one could see over castle walls.

As more manor houses became the norm, the popular landscape design changed. Structured gardens no longer were in style. An open lawn surrounded by a fence or hedge became the norm. The reason for this was the fact that people were entertaining more and lawn games were in vogue.

After Reformation, the concept of open space was still present but the open space was now converted to a park-like setting. While people still did enjoy the park setting, the main purpose for it was to protect deer and/or cattle behind a fenced off enclosure. While keeping your animals right against the house was not favorable, this type of landscape design was used beyond the home. Formal gardens were preferred around the manor house or castle. To keep some level of privacy, the landscaped area around the home is still encircled with a stone wall or hedge.

The Tudor and Stuart periods are the ones that had the most influence on the landscape design of Versailles. The characteristics of a Tudor landscape are knot gardens, which are encircled with a stone wall or hedge. The Stuart style continues with what the Tudors liked and adds a broad avenue from the house into the full length of the garden space. Stuart landscape design also favored parterres, which would line each side of the wide sidewalk.

What is a parterre? Well, in a nutshell, it is a knot garden without the walled outline. The plants are typically shrubs that are kept the same height. These shrubs form a pattern that is to be viewed from above. Knot gardens, on the other hand, consist of a hedge boarder around the design of the flower beds. This hedge acts more like a wall, and is normally taller than the other plants. The plants inside this outline are a parterre but the difference is the plant material is pruned to give the illusion that it is tied in a knot. To highlight the design, flowering plants and aromatics are placed in between the "knotted" plant material. Due to the pruning required for this type of design, boxwoods are normally the plant material used to tie the knot.

Paths in both parterres and knot gardens are normally made from gravel or stone paving.

During this same time period, Dutch influence on the landscape began to appear. Beyond the knot gardens and parterres, more elaborate water features appeared along with flowering bulbs. To control the environment even more, trees were not only planted in the ground but also in containers. Once trees and shrubs were planted in containers, the pruning and training of them into unnatural shapes followed. This gardening technique is referred to as topiaries.

The Tudor and Stuart time period influenced the landscape design of Versailles. In the 1630s, Louise the 13th made the final purchase of Versailles. Once that was done, Claude Mollet and Hilaire Masson where hired to design the formal gardens that were built west of the chateau. Not much beyond of the landscape design changed until Louise the 14th took over in the 1660s.

The chateau design along with the landscape changed once Louise the 14th inherited the property. In 1661, the first change occurred. Minor changes were made to the chateau but a lot of changes were in store for the landscaping. The first change came from the hiring of Andre Le Notre as the landscape architect. During this same time, Louis Le Vau designed the Versailles Orangery. The design of the orangery took advantage of a hilly area south of the chateau. This hilly space created a natural slope that protected the orange trees during the winter months.

In 1664, Louise the 14th was ready to show off his new gardens but he did learn of a fault in his building design. The problem was simple. There was not enough space in the chateau to house all his guests. If his friends and family wanted to stay another day to visit, they had to either go home and return or find an inn in a local village. To keep his guests there, Louise the 14th spurred on the second building campaign.

As the chateau was expanding so was the garden space. What the second building campaign meant for the gardens was fountains, bosquets, and garden art, which showed the relationship that Louise the 14th had with Apollo and the Sun. The solar images were simple support to the claim that Louise the 14th was the sun god.

While there did bosquets exist on the property, Andre Le Notre really took this landscape element to a new level. The bosquet is a grove of trees the same species that are planted in a row or in an orchard style. Another design of a bosquet is to plant five trees the same species in a cross shape with the fifth tree becoming the center of the cross. This type of planting is called quincunx. To keep the trees looking uniform, the lower branches are pruned to the same level. The trunks of these trees may be washed with lime to showcase the identical trunks. These trees may also be pleached, which is technique where the branches of the trees are weaved together to form living fences, shaded walks or allies.

The understory of the bosquet could be left grassy or covered in stone but another approach is to have a hedge of shrubs growing underneath the trees. This technique is one that Andre Le Notre encouraged. Bosquets combined with palisades helped create the concept of "closet of greenery." This "closet of greenery" shaped a room out of the grove of trees that had one way in and out along a path. In the center of the "room" typically was garden art. This gave the feeling of privacy and bloomed into an idea, which treated the landscape as additional living space to be enjoyed.

Not much changed during Louise the 15th 60 year reign. When Louise the 16th came into power, the beginning of garden renovation started to occur. What created this change was two-fold. First, Louise the 15th liked to spend money. And two, the gardens needed upkeep. In doing so, many trees were felled during this time period. This was not due to a remodeling of the gardens but needed to be done for the health of the garden space. Since the Sun King's reign, many of the plants especially the trees had not been maintained. Many trees had become overgrown and diseased. To preserve the garden space, the removal of diseased plant material was a top priority.

While the garden cleanup was going on, a garden transformation was occurring. French garden design was no longer desired at Versailles. English gardens were more Louise the 16th taste. So as the diseased trees were removed, the gardens were being converted to English garden design. But the landscape itself had different plans. Due to the topography of Versailles, the English garden design was not possible and the hope of converting the gardens of Versailles into an English garden showpiece was dashed. Many of the converted gardens were repurposed back into French garden design.

Whereas Louise the 16th liked to spend money, he knew that finances needed to be saved somewhere. To cut down on the maintenance cost of the gardens, ordered the palissades to be removed, which were the finely pruned shrubs that formed the walls in the bosquet. To fill in these spaces lime or chestnut trees were planted in rows.

As a result of the French Revolution, trees were chopped down but there were those who saw the value of saving the gardens of Versailles. While the removal of the trees where directed by the National Convention, Louise Claude Maria Richard lobbied convinced this same organization to save them. He promoted the historical value of the gardens and offered alternative uses such as opening the gardens to the public and planting vegetable in the spaces where parterres were located. While the gardens were opened to the public-and still are, the plans for the vegetable gardens never materialized.

Napoleon Bonaparte was not concerned with the garden space as far as maintenance but he did have some tree felled. Due to the removal of the trees, soil erosion became a problem. To fix the soil erosion problem, the trees were replanted.

Louie the 18th once again tried to convert some of the gardens into English gardens. While this conversation occurred in 1817 by 1892, a new concept was taking hold. Pierre de Nolhac was the director of the museum whose job it was to protect all of Versailles. To do this, the history of Versailles had to be pieced together. From this information, guidelines for restoration where established for the building and gardens. This restoration effort continues today with an eye on letting the gardens tell the story of Versailles instead of planting what is in vogue.

Creating A Tabletop Knot Garden

As one can image, knot gardens were a status symbol for the royal class of the past. During this time period, every grand home had a knot garden and every garden had a wide variety of skilled workers who took care of the garden. While knot gardens do require daily maintenance, today's knot garden can be planned in a way that reduces some of the work.

A knot garden is a wonderful lesson in geometry and illusion. The concept of a knot garden is to utilize the different textures and shades of plant material to create the "threads" of a living tapestry. These "threads" are then interwoven to give the illusion that one thread is passing under another in the form of a knot.

During the 14th and 15th century, two different styles of knot gardens were created. An open design is one by which you could see paths. The closed design occurs when the garden space is completely filled in with plants.

Any knot garden begins with a plan. While the visual concept of "tying" plants into knot may seem a little advanced for this time period, many experts believe the knot garden idea came from observing tapestries. The complicated knots that were used to create the designs where mimicked on the ground as knot gardens. Though you may not have any tapestries sitting around, you can find inspiration by looking at existing knot gardens found in Europe. Or, check out some books on knot gardens. If you are really adventurous, create a garden design from an existing knot such as a clover hitch, overhand or figure eight knot. If you are not a great artist, do not worry. Simply trace the knot and enlarge it on graph paper to the size of 18 by 18-inch box, which will be discussed later.

Once the design is created, the fun begins. Now is the time to play around with color and design. Since we are going to create a tabletop version of a knot garden, the plants needed are herbs and small flowering plants. To aid in plant design, follow this knot garden rule of thumb. When it comes to straight lines in your design, reserve the plants that come in shades of green, gray or purple for this use.

After you have picked several plants that you would like to use in your knot garden, add this information to the plan. Color-code the area where each plant will be located and take a look at your design from above. Continue to play around with the plant material until you find a combination that you like.

Once you have created a design you like, including shape and plant material, the next step is deciding on how much plant material you will need. If the design was done on graph paper, you can count the squares and then at least double the plant material. The reason for this is the fact that the plant material is spaced closer so that the knot forms quicker.

Another note about plant selection- herbs are perfect for a tabletop knot garden. These plants are used to excessive pruning and are easily found in small sizes, which is important for this container garden. Remember though that you will still need to know where the knot garden is going so that you can choose the proper plants that meet the environmental conditions.

Building the Box

Supplies

6 board feet of 1 x 6 untreated wood

Box of screws

Chicken wire

Landscape cloth

Scissors

Wire snips

Staple gun with staples

Steps

1. Cut boards into four 18-inch long pieces
2. Take two pieces of the wood and screw together into a L-shape.
3. Add another board to the L-shape and screw together.
4. Complete the container frame by screwing the last piece of wood.
5. Decide which side of the container will be the top.
6. Flip the box so that the bottom is facing up. Measure the bottom of the box and cut a piece of chicken wire that size.
7. Attach chicken wire to the bottom of the box with staples.
8. Measure the inside of the box and cut a piece of landscape cloth the same size.
9. Place the landscape cloth inside the box and fill with a good all-purpose soil.

10. Gently tap the box on the table and add more soil as needed to get the soil level within ¾ to ½ inch from the top.

Planting the Box

1. Begin the planting process by first getting your design on the soil surface. This can be done by mapping out the design with pencils, string and powdered milk.
2. Once the design is on the soil's surface, begin the planting process. The best approach is to start in the middle and work your way out. When it comes to actually planting the plants, gently remove the plant from its container and remove some of the soil from around the roots. Next, dig a hole in the soil and place the appropriate plant in that space. Gently push the soil around the roots and repeat by placing the plants every two to three inches.
3. When it comes to the straight line plants, prune them to the same height and then plant as described above. To keep the line straight, consider taking a stake and using it as a straight edge guide by which you will follow. Following this straight edge, create a trench by digging the soil with a spoon.
4. Whenever the plants enter an intersection, a small space will need to be made. This will aid in the up and down illusion of the knot and make pruning easier.
5. Once all the plants have been planted, water the design in.
6. To conserve soil moisture, cover the bare soil with any type of mulch

7. Continue to monitor the soil moisture and water when the soil feels dry.
8. In about three weeks, your tabletop knot garden will begin to explode with growth and the design will begin to show. Continue to prune throughout the growing season and fertilize with a water-soluble fertilizer in a balanced formulation such as a 10-10-10.

ADDENDUM

My great-grandmother's relationship with me continued to bloom while I was at Purdue. By this time, my great-grandfather had passed and she was faced with a whole new world. As an example, I would get letters from her while my great-grandfather was still alive; the frequency of those letters diminished after his passing. Why was that? The answer was so simple. She viewed herself as inferior to anyone with an education--which my great-grandfather had. While it was just a high school diploma, she always felt her written word was not worth reading. This would change sooner than I wanted it to.

Two years after my great-grandfather died, my great-grandmother had a stroke. As her health declined, so did her magical garden. There really seemed to be some type of symbiotic relationship between my great-grandmother and the garden she loved so dearly. As the weeds took over the garden space, cobwebs seemed to cloud her mind. A mind that knew the genealogy of every plant she ever planted in her garden, along with all the who, when and where about each plant.

Then it happened.

The phone rang with the news of the death of my family's gardening monarch.

I was summoned to Lexington, Kentucky for my great-grandmother's funeral. I could hear my great-grandmother complaining about the dead flowers. No, she was not a complainer, but she would have felt that the death of all these flowers was not warranted. I mean, everyone dies--she would say. She always viewed placing dead flowers around a person was really kind of odd. Why she would ask? Do not pick the flowers for me. Instead, allow them to grow and color the world with their beauty. You know, I have to agree with her.

After the funeral, my grandmother pulled me to the side. She needed me to come by my great-grandmother's home and pick something up. She made a point to tell me that my great-grandmother had left something for me, but I was not to tell anyone. The truth was I was the only great-grandchild she left anything to.

As I drove up the steep driveway, I could envision my little, independent great-grandmother walking down the driveway with her purse on her arm and a plan for when she caught the bus to go to town. Was this vision when she went to town with her sewing money in hand to buy her engagement ring? Which my great-grandfather felt was such a waste--or was it the razor when she wanted to shave her legs? Well, it really did not matter. I could see her one more time--even if it was just in my head.

Or was it?

When I reached the porch of the house, my grandmother met me with a box. Oh this box was unique! It was worn--I mean really worn. You know the kind of worn that something gets when it is really loved. For the life of me, I could not figure out why she left me this box. As I thought about the day's events, I found myself in my great-grandmother's garden. The enchanted garden that in the past had twinkled with a rainbow of colors was now brown and overgrown to the point that I did not even recognize it. I worked my way through the overgrowth and found a clearing near the dry stonewall that was in the back of the garden. I sat there for awhile thinking about the events of the past few months and contemplated what was in the box. A simple wooden box that I could tell had been loved so much.

I do not know how much time passed; I began to see the color of the sky change. The sun was setting, and I really needed to leave. While my mind was telling me to get up, my body just would not move. I felt that to move forward figuratively and emotionally, I needed to open the box.

The lid of the box seemed to have a life of its own. I mean I do not remember opening up the latch in the front and lifting the lid. But there it was open. I was puzzled by what I saw. A neatly folded piece of paper was on top. Odd, I thought. I opened it up. I immediately recognized the handwriting. It was my great-grandmother, Emma Jean Franklin. In the letter, she explained to me what was inside and apologized for its contents. You see, what was inside was her most prized possession from a man that felt an engagement ring was a waste of money. This man was my great-grandfather, James Louis Franklin. During my great-grandparents early marriage, my great-grandmother would toll in the garden with a spoon. Yes, I said a spoon. I suppose when you are that poor a spoon is better than a stick. When it came to trees though, Papaw Franklin would dig the hole with a shovel he borrowed from a neighbor. As the years went by and finances were better, Papaw Franklin bought himself a shovel. But Grannie Franklin continued to use her spoon. Then in 1938 things changed. My great-grandfather had a good-paying job through the railroad and they seemed to be living on easy street.

Now, I know that wealth is short-lived. I mean WWII was just around the corner, but they did not know that at the time. My great-grandfather felt it was time to get Emma Jean something beyond a spoon to use in her garden. So with cash in hand, he went to a blacksmith that he had met on the railroad, and commissioned him to make hand-forged gardening tools for his true love. Since my great-grandmother was so used to using a spoon, he felt that hand tools would be perfect. In doing so, he had a hand spade, cultivator, and rake made. To make it easy on Emma Jean's hands, he had the handles made from oak. Since there was a little oak leftover, the blacksmith make a dibbler for her, so she could stop using her finger to gauge seed depth.

The letter continued, but I felt the need to stop reading it--plus the light was fading. As I moved my hand through the box, I came upon something wrapped in one of my great-grandmother's hand-embroidered--and tattered--handkerchiefs. When the weather was too cold to garden, she would sit in her sitting room and decorate her new handkerchiefs to add to her wardrobe. The theme of the embroidery was always the same and included the new plants in her garden. Once this memory elapsed, I moved on to unwrap the small package. Underneath the handkerchief was my great-grandmother's hand spade. This process was repeated for each item in the box. As I gently handled each item, there was something odd about the handles--they were worn from wear. The protective finish had long--ago worn off, but they just did not feel right. I laid the box down and went to my car. Searching for paper, I could not find any, but I found a pencil. I went back to the dry stonewall and thought about what could be wrong with the handles. As I looked at the letter that Emma Jean had written me, I noticed that the page was not completely filled. Oh, how I wanted to keep this letter but my desire to understand the handles was strong. The pull to put the paper on a handle and rub it with the pencil--like a tombstone etching--seemed to come from somewhere else outside myself. Not being able to resist the urge, I put paper to handle and pencil to paper. Then, I began to rub.

It did not take much time before I figured out what was wrong with the handles. There really was nothing wrong--but love. You see, Papaw Franklin had each one of the handles engraved with the following.

To my only love, Emma Jean Franklin

From James Louis Franklin

February 14, 1938

As I laid out this labor of love on the top of the dry stonewall, I began to realize the true love and sacrifice these simple gardening tools represented. After contemplating the contents of the box and all that I had discovered, I looked up and saw my great-grandmother standing outside her mudroom, apron on, ready to garden. She gave me a head nod and dissolved into the shadows of the quickly-approaching nightfall. How I did not want to leave. But I knew I needed to get the contents of the box back inside and make my way back to Indiana.

I realize now, and I suppose I always knew why, she left me her gardening tools. To anyone else, the box would have been viewed as broken, dirty, and tattered. The contents would have been seen as not worth much; and frankly, just some garden junk. To me, though, it was the symbol of a life, hard work, and true love that never died.

Today, my great-grandmother's enchanted garden is part of what some people call "progress," which equates out to mean--another house. While that garden is lost, I have my own--by which I have taught my kids to garden. I also have the privilege of teaching people the long lost art of gardening as a profession. Throughout my gardening journey, I am always thinking about Emma Jean's wisdom. The world of gardening is one that my great-grandmother would not recognize. Computers, computer games, and virtual reality allow people to experience gardening without ever walking outside... but nothing beats the feel of soil underneath your fingernails and the love permeating the soul through one of Emma Jean's hand tools.

The gardening story continues..........

ACKNOWLEDGEMENTS

While I would love to give credit to all those involved in my life that made this project possible, there is not enough space or time. In just, I would like to thank all those mentioned and thought of in my heart as the support system that made writing this book a reality.

The first person I would like to thank is Diane Gabaldon, the author of the Outlander book series. Without her creativity and eye for detail, this book would have never been possible. Nor would the world's eyes be open to a world that many people have forgotten about and/or never knew existed.

My dad is the second person by which I would like to thank. The conception of the book came from my dad and I watching an episode of Outlander on STARZ at his house. While I would have preferred a different episode, it just happened to be the Black Jack Randall and Jamie rape storyline that my dad and I watched that faithful evening. While embarrassed by the topic, the lavender oil peaked my interest and this is when the book idea entered my life. When I threw out the book idea to my dad, he told me to just go for it. Whereas I do not know if he really could envision what I was talking about, his support gave me the courage to move on in the process.

The third person I would like to thank is my husband, Steve Shetter Jr. He has lived through many of my projects and is one that I go to when I have a technology issue. Without his patience with technology, this book and the YouTube channel would not have been possible.

I would also like to thank my custom costume designer Suzan van Breda from Tenez Ferme for her hard work in creating this beautiful Outlander inspired time period costume by which I use for the videos. Another invaluable person I would like to thank is Kerry Robinson at Kerry Illustrate. Through our many Internet conversations, she was able to take my ideas and turn them into reality. While the challenge was vast and covered two continents, Kerry creatively designed a book cover along with hand drawn sketches that really make the book feel like a loved piece of botanical equipment that was carried, used, and loved in the 1740s.

Another person I would like to thank is Deborah Aubrey-Peyron author of the *Miraculous Interventions* Book series. Through her guidance and editing, she also helped me make my vision become reality.

Finally, I would like to thank my feet. Yes, I said my feet. They have comfortably carried me through this book's journey and over many miles of thought while I worked out the details of the book. Without their constant support, my periods of walking meditation would have never been possible. In doing so, the book concept would have never seen full sun in my garden of ideas.

AUTHOR BIO

Mindy McIntosh-Shetter is an agricultural blogger and video blogger (vlogger) who shares her gardening knowledge through several companies, including an online gardening magazine, The Weekend Gardener. Her vast knowledge is an accumulation of life experiences and Bachelor of Science degree in Agriculture Education, with a minor in biology from Purdue University, along with a Masters of Arts in Interdisciplinary Studies from the University of Louisville.

A new approach to gardening is the field of historical botany combining ethnobotany and gardening with a story. Utilizing her educational background, Mindy has found an interest and intriguing way of reaching history lovers, gardeners, and the famous Outlander lovers.

As an environmentalist at heart, she specializes in teaching people how to garden organically. While encouraging those who think they cannot garden to take spade to the soil, regardless if you are an urban or landless gardener. While her goal is to have a hologram that can go out into the garden and garden with you, technology has just not caught up. To meet this need, check out Outlander Botanist YouTube channel along with the Outlander Botanist website. Continue the conversation with other like-minded people by subscribing to the Outlander Botanist on Facebook and Twitter .

400 Guild Videography

REFERENCES

While many may scuff at using Internet sources as references, this was a deliberate act. I wanted the reader not to have to buy a book mentioned as a reference if they wanted to explore the plant material beyond the scope of this book. Every effort has been made to use reliable sources, such as Extension publications and WebMD for medical uses of the plants.

The references are arranged by the sections of the book and aphetically when it comes to the plant material. Some of the references are also source of plant or seed material. This is not an endorsement of any company.

Please note: if you would like an interactive reference list, please check out the Outlander Botanist website.

Intro web information

http://www.science20.com/humboldt_fellow_and_science/blog/intimate_relationship_between_human_and_plant_world_has_evolved_over_generations_experience_pra

Intro web information

http://www.washacadsci.org/Journal/Journalarticles/V.90-3-Plants%20and%20Man%20in%20Antiquity-%20A%20Detective%20Story.Alain%20Touwaide.pdf

Getting to the basics
http://articles.mercola.com/sites/articles/archive/2016/02/22/dirt-cure-healthy-soil.aspx

Getting to the basics

http://content.ces.ncsu.edu/overcoming-seed-dormancy-trees-and-shrubs

Getting to the basics

http://planthardiness.ars.usda.gov/PHZMWeb/

Agrimony info:

http://hermionesgarden.blogspot.com/2011/02/agrimonia-eupatoria-agrimony.html

http://www.botanical-online.com/english/agrimonycultivation.htm

http://www.heirloom-organics.com/guide/va/guidetogrowingagrimony.html

http://www.webmd.com/vitamins-supplements/ingredientmono-491-agrimony.aspx?activeIngredientId=491&activeIngredientName=agrimony&source=1

Aloe info:

http://www.almanac.com/plant/aloe-vera

http://worldofsucculents.com/grow-care-aloe-vera/

http://www.webmd.com/vitamins-supplements/ingredientmono-607-ALOE.aspx?activeIngredientId=607&activeIngredientName=ALOE

http://umm.edu/health/medical/altmed/herb/aloe

http://homeguides.sfgate.com/propagate-aloe-vera-41646.html

Angelica info:

http://www.bhg.com/gardening/plant-dictionary/herb/angelica/

https://www.botanical.com/botanical/mgmh/a/anegl037.html#pro

http://www.ourherbgarden.com/angelica.html

http://www.missouribotanicalgarden.org/PlantFinder/PlantFinderDetails.aspx?kempercode=e399

http://www.ourherbgarden.com/herb-history/angelica.html

http://www.ourherbgarden.com/angelica-companions.html

http://www.heirloom-organics.com/guide/va/guidetogrowingangelica.html

http://www.webmd.com/vitamins-supplements/ingredientmono-281-angelica.aspx?activeIngredientId=281&activeIngredientName=angelica&source=1

Anise info:

http://www.usagardener.com/how_to_grow_herbs/how_to_grow_anise.php

http://www.harvesttotable.com/2009/04/how_to_grow_anise/

http://www.webmd.com/vitamins-supplements/ingredientmono-582-ANISE.aspx?activeIngredientId=582&activeIngredientName=ANISE

https://www.botanical.com/botanical/mgmh/a/anise040.html

http://www.motherearthnews.com/organic-gardening/growing-anise-in-the-herb-garden-zmaz82ndzgoe.aspx?PageId=1

http://www.heirloom-organics.com/guide/va/guidetogrowinganise.html

Basil info:

http://www.almanac.com/plant/basil

http://www.whfoods.com/genpage.php?tname=foodspice&dbid=85

http://www.offthegridnews.com/alternative-health/medicinal-uses-and-health-benefits-of-basil/

http://www.heirloom-organics.com/guide/va/guidetogrowingbasil.html

Bay leaf Info:

http://www.gardeningknowhow.com/edible/herbs/bay/sweet-bay-leaf-tree.htm

http://homeguides.sfgate.com/root-bay-leaf-cutting-38322.html

http://www.herbwisdom.com/herb-bay.html

http://www.rodalesorganiclife.com/garden/flower-power-bay-laurel

Betony info:

http://www.heirloom-organics.com/guide/va/guidetogrowingwoodbetony.html

http://www.motherearthliving.com/plant-profile/wood-betony.aspx

https://www.botanical.com/botanical/mgmh/b/betowo35.html

http://www.webmd.com/vitamins-supplements/ingredientmono-587-betony.aspx?activeIngredientId=587&activeIngredientName=betony&source=1&tabno=2

Bistort info:

http://www.pfaf.org/user/Plant.aspx?LatinName=Polygonum+bistorta

http://www.thegardenhelper.com/knotweed.html

http://www.herbs2000.com/herbs/herbs_bistort.htm

http://www.finegardening.com/bistort-persicaria-amplexicaulis

http://www.webmd.com/vitamins-supplements/ingredientmono-75-bistort.aspx?activeIngredientId=75&activeIngredientName=bistort&source=1&tabno=2

http://www.seedaholic.com/persicaria-bistorta-superba.html

Bladderwort info:

http://www.webmd.com/vitamins-supplements/ingredientmono-317-bladderwort.aspx?activeIngredientId=317&activeIngredientName=bladderwort&source=1

http://www.fs.fed.us/wildflowers/plant-of-the-week/utricularia_macrorhiza.shtml

http://littleshopofhorrors.co.uk/bladderwort.html

http://www.growcarnivorousplants.com/Articles.asp?ID=264

http://www.carnivorousplantnursery.com/info/growingbladderwort.htm

Bloodwort info:

http://www.earthclinic.com/remedies/bloodroot.html

http://www.bhg.com/gardening/plant-dictionary/perennial/bloodroot/

http://www.gardeningknowhow.com/ornamental/flowers/bloodroot/how-to-grow-bloodroot.htm

http://www.gardenguides.com/69703-grow-bloodroot.html

http://www.webmd.com/vitamins-supplements/ingredientmono-893-BLOODROOT.aspx?activeIngredientId=893&activeIngredientName=BLOODROOT

Bogbean info:

http://www.gardenershq.com/Menyanthes-Bog-Bean.php

http://www.pondsplantsandmore.com/Bog_Bean_Menyanthes_trifoliata_Marginal_Bog_p/pmh_bogbean.htm

http://www.pfaf.org/user/Plant.aspx?LatinName=Menyanthes+trifoliata

http://nationalpondservice.com/water-plant-buck-bean/

http://www.herbs2000.com/herbs/herbs_bogbean.htm

http://www.webmd.com/vitamins-supplements/ingredientmono-74-bogbean.aspx?activeIngredientId=74&activeIngredientName=bogbean&source=1&tabno=2

Boneset info:

http://www.heirloom-organics.com/guide/va/guidetogrowingboneset.html

http://www.gardenershq.com/Eupatorium-mist-flower.php

http://homeguides.sfgate.com/grow-eupatorium-38467.html

http://www.outsidepride.com/seed/flower-seed/eupatorium/eupatorium-boneset.html

http://www.webmd.com/vitamins-supplements/ingredientmono-594-boneset.aspx?activeIngredientId=594&activeIngredientName=boneset&source=1&tabno=2

Borage info:

http://herbgardening.com/growingborage.htm

Borage info:

http://www.usagardener.com/how_to_grow_herbs/how_to_grow_borage.php

Borage info:

http://www.webmd.com/vitamins-supplements/ingredientmono-596-borage.aspx?activeIngredientId=596&activeIngredientName=borage&source=1

https://www.botanical.com/botanical/mgmh/b/borage66.html

Bugloss info:

http://www.medicinalherbinfo.org/herbs/Borage.html

Burdock info:

http://herbgardens.about.com/od/medicinalherbs/p/Burdock-What-Is-Burdock.htm

http://www.heirloom-organics.com/guide/va/guidetogrowingburdock.html

http://www.webmd.com/vitamins-supplements/ingredientmono-111-burdock.aspx?activeIngredientId=111&activeIngredientName=burdock&source=1&tabno=2

http://countrywoodsmoke.com/burdock-leaf-bbq-lemon-sole/

Butterbur info:

http://www.missouribotanicalgarden.org/PlantFinder/PlantFinderDetails.aspx?kempercode=a645

http://www.herbs2000.com/herbs/herbs_butterbur.htm

http://www.pfaf.org/user/Plant.aspx?LatinName=Petasites+hybridus

http://www.pfaf.org/user/Plant.aspx?LatinName=Petasites+japonicus

http://www.webmd.com/vitamins-supplements/ingredientmono-649-butterbur.aspx?activeIngredientId=649&activeIngredientName=butterbur&source=1&tabno=2

Camomile or Chamomile info:

http://www.gardeningknowhow.com/edible/herbs/chamomile/growing-chamomile.htm

http://herbgardening.com/growingchamomile.htm

http://www.gardenguides.com/67596-grow-chamomile-indoors.html

http://www.webmd.com/vitamins-supplements/ingredientmono-951-Chamomile+GERMAN+CHAMOMILE.aspx?activeIngredientId=951&activeIngredientName=Chamomile+(GERMAN+CHAMOMILE)&source=2

http://www.webmd.com/vitamins-supplements/ingredientmono-752-Chamomile+ROMAN+CHAMOMILE.aspx?activeIngredientId=752&activeIngredientName=Chamomile+(ROMAN+CHAMOMILE)&source=2

Caraway info:

http://www.heirloom-organics.com/guide/va/guidetogrowingcaraway.html

https://www.quickcrop.co.uk/learning/plant/caraway

http://www.herbs2000.com/herbs/herbs_caraway.htm

http://www.webmd.com/vitamins-supplements/ingredientmono-204-CARAWAY.aspx?activeIngredientId=204&activeIngredientName=CARAWAY

Cardamom info:

http://cardamomhq.com/cardamom-plant/

http://www.heirloom-organics.com/guide/va/guidetogrowingcardamom.html

http://www.gardenguides.com/94816-grow-cardamom.html

http://www.webmd.com/vitamins-supplements/ingredientmono-614-cardamom.aspx?activeIngredientId=614&activeIngredientName=cardamom&source=1

Cascara info:

http://www.gardenguides.com/taxonomy/cascara-buckthorn-frangula-purshiana/

https://www.for.gov.bc.ca/hfd/library/documents/treebook/cascara.htm

http://www.herbworld.com/learningherbs/CASCARA%20SAGRADA.pdf

http://www.pfaf.org/user/Plant.aspx?LatinName=Rhamnus+purshiana

http://www.webmd.com/vitamins-supplements/ingredientmono-773-cascara.aspx?activeIngredientId=773&activeIngredientName=cascara&source=1

Catnip info:

http://herbgardening.com/growingcatnip.htm

http://www.webmd.com/vitamins-supplements/ingredientmono-831-CATNIP.aspx?activeIngredientId=831&activeIngredientName=CATNIP

Chelidonium info:

http://www.pfaf.org/user/Plant.aspx?LatinName=Chelidonium+majus

http://www.globalhealingcenter.com/organic-herbs/growing-greater-celandine

Chelidonium info: http://www.gardeningknowhow.com/plant-problems/weeds/greater-celandine-plant.htm

http://worldoffloweringplants.com/grow-care-greater-celandine/

http://www.botanical.com/botanical/mgmh/c/celgre43.html

http://www.webmd.com/vitamins-supplements/ingredientmono-676-greater+celandine.aspx?activeIngredientId=676&activeIngredientName=greater+celandine&source=1

Chickweed info:

http://homeguides.sfgate.com/grow-chickweed-70081.html

http://www.gardenguides.com/79845-grow-chickweed.html

http://www.greenprophet.com/2010/01/chickweed-cultivate-grow-home/

http://www.webmd.com/vitamins-supplements/ingredientmono-622-chickweed.aspx?activeIngredientId=622&activeIngredientName=chickweed&source=1

Cinquefoil info:

http://www.telegraph.co.uk/gardening/howtogrow/3301265/How-to-grow-Potentilla.html

http://www.gardenguides.com/75763-grow-cinquefoil.html

http://www.herbs2000.com/herbs/herbs_cinquefoil.htm

http://www.finegardening.com/shrubby-cinquefoil-potentilla-fruticosa

http://www.pfaf.org/user/Plant.aspx?LatinName=Potentilla+reptans

http://www.webmd.com/vitamins-supplements/ingredientmono-132-Cinquefoil+EUROPEAN+FIVE-FINGER+GRASS.aspx?activeIngredientId=132&activeIngredientName=Cinquefoil+(EUROPEAN+FIVE-FINGER+GRASS)&source=2

http://www.alchemy-works.com/herb_cinquefoil.html

http://www.thegardenhelper.com/potentilla.htm

Coltsfoot info:

http://www.motherearthliving.com/plant-profile/an-herb-to-know-39.aspx?PageId=1

http://www.botanical.com/botanical/mgmh/c/coltsf88.html

http://www.gardeningknowhow.com/garden-how-to/soil-fertilizers/organic-coltsfoot-fertilizer.htm

http://www.fs.fed.us/database/feis/plants/forb/tusfar/all.html

http://www.herbs2000.com/herbs/herbs_coltsfoot.htm

http://www.pfaf.org/user/plant.aspx?LatinName=Tussilago+farfara

http://www.anniesremedy.com/chart_remedy.php?rem_ID=85

Comfrey info:

http://gardening.about.com/od/herbsatoz/p/Comfrey.htm

http://www.floralencounters.com/Seeds/seed_detail.jsp?grow=Comfrey&productid=1060

http://www.finegardening.com/grow-more-plants-root-cuttings

http://www.seedaholic.com/symphytum-officinale-comfrey.html

http://www.grit.com/farm-and-garden/comfrey-tea-the-best-organic-fertilizer.aspx

http://www.herbs2000.com/herbs/herbs_comfrey.htm

http://www.motherearthnews.com/organic-gardening/comfrey-leaves-zmaz74zhol.aspx

http://www.webmd.com/vitamins-supplements/ingredientmono-295-comfrey.aspx?activeIngredientId=295&activeIngredientName=comfrey&source=1

Coneflower info:

http://www.herbs2000.com/herbs/herbs_echinacea.htm

http://www.almanac.com/plant/coneflowers

http://www.rodalesorganiclife.com/garden/grow-your-own-echinacea

https://umm.edu/health/medical/altmed/herb/echinacea

http://www.webmd.com/cold-and-flu/cold-guide/echinacea-common-cold

Corydalis info:

http://www.herbs2000.com/herbs/herbs_corydalis.htm

http://www.bhg.com/gardening/plant-dictionary/perennial/corydalis/

http://www.finegardening.com/corydalis

http://www.gardenershq.com/Corydalis-Fumitory.php

http://www.thegardenhelper.com/corydalis.html

http://www.webmd.com/vitamins-supplements/ingredientmono-415-corydalis.aspx?activeIngredientId=415&activeIngredientName=corydalis&source=1

Cow parsley info:

http://www.seedaholic.com/anthriscus-sylvestris-cow-parsley.html

http://www.onlyfoods.net/cow-parsley.html

http://www.independent.co.uk/voices/comment/cow-parsley-the-countryside-killer-9397226.html

https://en.wikipedia.org/wiki/Anthriscus_sylvestris

http://www.pfaf.org/user/Plant.aspx?LatinName=Anthriscus+sylvestris

http://www.voyageurcountry.com/htmls/floweringplants/plants/queenanneslace.html

Dandelion info:

http://www.gardeningknowhow.com/edible/vegetables/greens/growing-dandelion.htm

http://www.heirloom-organics.com/guide/va/guidetogrowingdandelion.html

http://www.webmd.com/vitamins-supplements/ingredientmono-706-dandelion.aspx?activeIngredientId=706&activeIngredientName=dandelion&source=1

Dill info:

http://www.almanac.com/plant/dill

http://herbgardening.com/growingdill.htm

http://www.extension.umn.edu/garden/yard-garden/vegetables/dill/

http://www.webmd.com/vitamins-supplements/ingredientmono-463-dill.aspx?activeIngredientId=463&activeIngredientName=dill&source=1

Dittany info:

http://davesgarden.com/guides/pf/go/53014/

http://www.gardeningknowhow.com/edible/herbs/dittany-of-crete/dittany-crete-herb-info.htm

http://www.herbnet.com/DITTANY%20OF%20CRETE.pdf

Dock info:

http://www.rootsimple.com/2013/12/campfire-cooking-fish-in-clay-vegetarian-options/

http://www.gardenershq.com/Rumex-Sorrel.php

http://www.ediblewildfood.com/yellow-dock.aspx

http://horticulture.oregonstate.edu/content/broadleaf-dock

http://returntonature.us/stalking-the-curly-dock-rumex-crispus/

http://www.botanical.com/botanical/mgmh/d/docks-15.html

Dropwort info:

http://www.gardeningknowhow.com/ornamental/flowers/dropwort/how-to-grow-dropworts.htm

http://www.webmd.com/vitamins-supplements/ingredientmono-108-Dropwort+MEADOWSWEET.aspx?activeIngredientId=108&activeIngredientName=Dropwort+(MEADOWSWEET)&source=2

Elecampane info:

http://www.herbs2000.com/herbs/herbs_elecampane.htm

http://valleyseedco.com/11830/growing-elecampane/

http://www.gardenershq.com/Inula-Elecampane.php

http://www.botanical.com/botanical/mgmh/e/elecam07.html

http://www.digthedirt.com/plants/15406-herbs-inula-helenium

http://gaiasworld.com/HR_E.html

http://www.webmd.com/vitamins-supplements/ingredientmono-2-elecampane.aspx?activeIngredientId=2&activeIngredientName=elecampane&source=1

Eyebright info:

http://homeguides.sfgate.com/grow-eyebright-27411.html

http://www.greenchronicle.com/gardening/eyebright_herb.htm

http://www.anniesremedy.com/herb_detail202.php

https://www.botanical.com/botanical/mgmh/e/eyebri20.html

http://www.webmd.com/vitamins-supplements/ingredientmono-109-eyebright.aspx?activeIngredientId=109&activeIngredientName=eyebright&source=1

Fennel info:

http://www.heirloom-organics.com/guide/va/guidetogrowingfennel.html

http://herbgardening.com/growingfennel.htm

http://www.vegetablegardener.com/item/4285/how-to-grow-herb-fennel

http://www.medicalnewstoday.com/articles/284096.php

http://www.webmd.com/vitamins-supplements/ingredientmono-311-FENNEL.aspx?activeIngredientId=311&activeIngredientName=FENNEL

Foxglove info:

http://www.gardeningknowhow.com/ornamental/flowers/foxglove/foxglove-flowers.htm

http://www.thompson-morgan.com/growing-foxgloves-from-seed

http://www.bhg.com/gardening/plant-dictionary/perennial/foxglove/

http://www.mda.state.mn.us/plants/pestmanagement/weedcontrol/noxiouslist/foxglove.aspx

https://www.botanical.com/botanical/mgmh/f/foxglo30.html

http://www.naturalremedies.org/foxglove/

http://www.webmd.com/vitamins-supplements/ingredientmono-287-foxglove.aspx?activeIngredientId=287&activeIngredientName=foxglove&source=1

Fumitory info:

http://www.herbs2000.com/herbs/herbs_fumitory.htm

http://www.botanical.com/botanical/mgmh/f/fumito36.html

http://davesgarden.com/guides/articles/view/2170/

http://www.indianmirror.com/ayurveda/fumitory.html

http://www.webmd.com/vitamins-supplements/ingredientmono-451-fumitory.aspx?activeIngredientId=451&activeIngredientName=fumitory&source=1

http://archive.lls.nsw.gov.au/__data/assets/pdf_file/0007/495349/archive-fumitory.pdf

Gentian info:

http://gentian.rutgers.edu/garden.htm

http://www.gardenersworld.com/how-to/grow-plants/how-to-take-cuttings-from-alpines/

http://www.telegraph.co.uk/gardening/howtogrow/3299785/How-to-grow-gentiana.html

http://davesgarden.com/guides/articles/view/827/

http://www.bhg.com/gardening/plant-dictionary/perennial/gentian/

http://botanical.com/botanical/mgmh/g/gentia08.html

http://www.webmd.com/vitamins-supplements/ingredientmono-716-GENTIAN.aspx?activeIngredientId=716&activeIngredientName=GENTIAN

Germander info:

http://www.motherearthliving.com/Gardening/Please-Bees-with-Germander.aspx

http://www.bhg.com/gardening/plant-dictionary/perennial/germander/

http://www.gardenershq.com/Teucrium-germander.php

http://homeguides.sfgate.com/grow-germander-38774.html

http://www.mountainvalleygrowers.com/teuchamaedrys.htm

http://www.botanical.com/botanical/mgmh/g/gerwat12.html

http://www.webmd.com/vitamins-supplements/ingredientmono-70-germander.aspx?activeIngredientId=70&activeIngredientName=germander&source=1

Ginger info:

http://www.gardening-guides.com/novelties/ginger.php

http://homeguides.sfgate.com/grow-ginger-plant-indoors-during-winter-44013.html

http://herbgardens.about.com/od/indoorgardening/a/How-Can-I-Grow-My-Own-Ginger-Root-Indoors.htm

http://homeguides.sfgate.com/planting-zones-ginger-root-65239.html

http://www.webmd.com/vitamins-supplements/ingredientmono-961-ginger.aspx?activeIngredientId=961&activeIngredientName=ginger&source=1

Goldenrod info:

http://www.herbco.com/c-347-goldenrod.aspx

Goldenrod info:

http://plants.usda.gov/plantguide/pdf/pg_sose.pdf

https://www.plants.usda.gov/core/profile?symbol=SOLID

https://www.nature.org/ourinitiatives/regions/northamerica/unitedstates/indiana/journeywithnature/shorts-goldenrod.xml

http://www.webmd.com/vitamins-supplements/ingredientmono-84-goldenrod.aspx?activeIngredientId=84&activeIngredientName=goldenrod&source=1

Goldenseal info:

http://www.grit.com/farm-and-garden/goldenseal-herb-rare-but-can-be-cultivated-for-profit-and-health.aspx

http://www.ginsengseed.com/goldinstructions2.html

http://www.gardenguides.com/68969-grow-goldenseal.html

http://plants.usda.gov/plantguide/pdf/pg_hyca.pdf

http://articles.extension.org/pages/68255/goldenseal-hydrastis-canadensis-1

http://www.cloverleaffarmherbs.com/goldenseal/

http://www.johnnyseeds.com/herbs/goldenseal/goldenseal-organic-root-899.html

https://www.southernexposure.com/goldenseal-10-rhizomes-p-986.html

http://shadeflowers.com/

http://www.webmd.com/vitamins-supplements/ingredientmono-943-goldenseal.aspx?activeIngredientId=943&activeIngredientName=goldenseal&source=1

Goutweed info:

http://davesgarden.com/guides/pf/go/546/

http://www.botanical.com/botanical/mgmh/g/goutwe32.html

http://www.gardenershq.com/Aegopodium-Bishops-weed-Goutweed.php

http://www.webmd.com/vitamins-supplements/ingredientmono-22-GOUTWEED.aspx?activeIngredientId=22&activeIngredientName=GOUTWEED

Horehound info:

http://www.motherearthnews.com/organic-gardening/growing-white-horehound-in-the-herb-garden-zmaz85jazgoe.aspx

http://www.outsidepride.com/seed/flower-seed/horehound-flower-seed.html

http://theworldmostpopularherbs.blogspot.com/2012/01/horehound-marrubium-vulgare-health.html

http://www.webmd.com/vitamins-supplements/ingredientmono-886-Horehound+WHITE+HOREHOUND.aspx?activeIngredientId=886&activeIngredientName=Horehound+(WHITE+HOREHOUND)&source=2

Hyssop info:

http://www.gardening.cornell.edu/homegardening/scene825e.html

http://herbgardening.com/growinghyssop.htm

http://www.webmd.com/vitamins-supplements/ingredientmono-258-hyssop.aspx?activeIngredientId=258&activeIngredientName=hyssop&source=1

Lavender info:

http://www.herbs2000.com/herbs/herbs_lavender.htm

http://www.midwestliving.com/garden/flowers/how-to-grow-lavender/

https://bonnieplants.com/growing/growing-lavender/

http://herbgardening.com/growinglavender.htm

http://everything-lavender.com/growing-lavender-plants-from-seed.html

http://www.burpee.com/gardenadvicecenter/herbs/lavender/how-to-grow-lavender-from-seed/article10487.html

http://www.medicalnewstoday.com/articles/265922.php

http://aanos.org/human-male-sexual-response-to-olfactory-stimuli/

http://www.motherearthliving.com/Natural-Beauty/the-therapy-of-aroma

http://www.health.com/health/gallery/0,,20587573,00.html

http://www.webmd.com/vitamins-supplements/ingredientmono-838-LAVENDER.aspx?activeIngredientId=838&activeIngredientName=LAVENDER

Madder root info:

http://www.herbs2000.com/herbs/herbs_madder.htm

http://www.nytimes.com/2012/04/05/garden/a-new-generation-discovers-grow-it-yourself-dyes.html?_r=0

http://davesgarden.com/guides/pf/go/59686/

http://www.webmd.com/vitamins-supplements/ingredientmono-557-MADDER.aspx?activeIngredientId=557&activeIngredientName=MADDER

Mallow root info:

http://www.botanical.com/botanical/mgmh/m/mallow07.html

http://www.heirloom-organics.com/guide/va/guidetogrowingmarshmallow.html

http://www.webmd.com/vitamins-supplements/ingredientmono-774-MARSHMALLOW.aspx?activeIngredientId=774&activeIngredientName=MARSHMALLOW

Marjoram info:

http://herbgardening.com/growingmarjoram.htm

http://www.motherearthnews.com/organic-gardening/growing-your-own-marjoram-zmaz04jjzsel

http://www.heirloom-organics.com/guide/va/guidetogrowingmarjoram.html

http://www.webmd.com/vitamins-supplements/ingredientmono-563-marjoram.aspx?activeIngredientId=563&activeIngredientName=marjoram&source=1

Meadowsweet info:

http://www.bhg.com/gardening/plant-dictionary/perennial/meadowsweet/

http://www.telegraph.co.uk/gardening/howtogrow/3342950/How-to-grow-meadowsweet.html

http://www.motherearthliving.com/Plant-Profile/HERBS-TO-KNOW-Sweets-in-the-Garden-Three-Historic-Herbs

http://homeguides.sfgate.com/germination-meadowsweet-77955.html

http://www.webmd.com/vitamins-supplements/ingredientmono-108-meadowsweet.aspx?activeIngredientId=108&activeIngredientName=meadowsweet&source=1

Mint info:

http://www.bhg.com/gardening/vegetable/herbs/grow-mint-plants/#page=0

http://www.rodalesorganiclife.com/garden/mint-growing-guide

http://www.medicalnewstoday.com/articles/275944.php

Mullein info:

http://botanical.com/botanical/mgmh/m/mulgre63.html

http://www.heirloom-organics.com/guide/va/guidetogrowingmullein.html

http://www.bhg.com/gardening/plant-dictionary/perennial/mullein/

http://www.webmd.com/vitamins-supplements/ingredientmono-572-mullein.aspx?activeIngredientId=572&activeIngredientName=mullein&source=1

Mustard info:

http://www.webmd.com/vitamins-supplements/ingredientmono-590-Mustard++BLACK+MUSTARD.aspx?activeIngredientId=590&activeIngredientName=Mustard++(BLACK+MUSTARD)&source=2

http://www.webmd.com/vitamins-supplements/ingredientmono-115-Mustard++WHITE+MUSTARD.aspx?activeIngredientId=115&activeIngredientName=Mustard++(WHITE+MUSTARD)&source=2

http://www.heirloom-organics.com/guide/va/guidetogrowingmustard.html

http://www.harvesttotable.com/2009/02/how_to_grow_mustard/

Nettles info:

http://www.heirloom-organics.com/guide/va/guidetogrowingnettle.html

http://www.barbarapleasant.com/stingingnettles.html

http://umm.edu/health/medical/altmed/herb/stinging-nettle

http://www.webmd.com/vitamins-supplements/ingredientmono-664-STINGING%20NETTLE.aspx?activeIngredientId=664&activeIngredientName=STINGING%20NETTLE

Nightshade info:

http://homeguides.sfgate.com/nightshade-grow-82116.html

http://www.westonaprice.org/health-topics/nightshades/

http://mobi.spellsofmagic.com/read_article.html?a=1782

http://davesgarden.com/guides/pf/go/68211/

https://www.gardeningknowhow.com/plant-problems/weeds/get-rid-nightshade.htm

https://www.botanical.com/botanical/mgmh/n/nighde05.html

http://www.webmd.com/vitamins-supplements/ingredientmono-921-Nightshade+JIMSON+WEED.aspx?activeIngredientId=921&activeIngredientName=Nightshade+(JIMSON+WEED)&source=2

Nutmeg info:

http://www.ehow.com/how_7715619_grow-nutmeg-tree-seed.html

http://urbanfig.com/nutmeg-can-i-grow-it/

http://www.webmd.com/vitamins-supplements/ingredientmono-788-nutmeg.aspx?activeIngredientId=788&activeIngredientName=nutmeg&source=1

Orris root info:

http://www.herbs2000.com/herbs/herbs_orris_root.htm

http://www.life.ca/naturallife/9806/iris.htm

http://medicinalherbinfo.org/herbs/OrrisRoot.html

http://www.almanac.com/plant/irises

http://www.webmd.com/vitamins-supplements/ingredientmono-645-ORRIS.aspx?activeIngredientId=645&activeIngredientName=ORRIS

Parsley info:

http://www.almanac.com/plant/parsley

http://www.extension.umn.edu/garden/yard-garden/vegetables/growing-parsley/

http://www.webmd.com/vitamins-supplements/ingredientmono-792-PARSLEY.aspx?activeIngredientId=792&activeIngredientName=PARSLEY

http://www.medicalnewstoday.com/articles/284490.php

Pellitory-of-the-wall info:

http://pfaf.org/user/Plant.aspx?LatinName=Parietaria+officinalis

http://www.herbs2000.com/herbs/herbs_pellitory_wall.htm

http://www.botanical.com/botanical/mgmh/p/pelwal22.html

http://www.webmd.com/vitamins-supplements/ingredientmono-481-PELLITORY-OF-THE-WALL.aspx?activeIngredientId=481&activeIngredientName=PELLITORY-OF-THE-WALL

Pennyroyal info:

https://www.gardeningknowhow.com/edible/herbs/pennyroyal/growing-pennyroyal.htm

http://www.motherearthnews.com/natural-health/herbal-remedies/pennyroyal-safety

http://www.herbs2000.com/herbs/herbs_pennyroyal.htm

http://www.motherearthnews.com/natural-health/herbal-remedies/pennyroyal-safety

https://hort.purdue.edu/newcrop/HerbHunters/pennyroyal.html

http://www.webmd.com/vitamins-supplements/ingredientmono-480-pennyroyal.aspx?activeIngredientId=480&activeIngredientName=pennyroyal&source=1

Peppermint info:

http://www.gardenguides.com/481-growing-using-peppermint.html

http://www.motherearthnews.com/Organic-Gardening/Peppermint-Herb-Garden-zmaz81jazkin/

http://www.webmd.com/vitamins-supplements/ingredientmono-705-peppermint.aspx?activeIngredientId=705&activeIngredientName=peppermint&source=1

Plantain info:

http://www.heirloom-organics.com/guide/va/guidetogrowingplantain.html

http://www.heirloom-organics.com/guide/va/guidetogrowingplantain.html

http://www.outsidepride.com/seed/herb-seed/plantain/plantain-common.html

http://www.webmd.com/vitamins-supplements/ingredientmono-677-Plantain+GREAT+PLANTAIN.aspx?activeIngredientId=677&activeIngredientName=Plantain+(GREAT+PLANTAIN)&source=2

http://www.webmd.com/vitamins-supplements/ingredientmono-347-Plantain+WATER+PLANTAIN.aspx?activeIngredientId=347&activeIngredientName=Plantain+(WATER+PLANTAIN)&source=2

http://www.webmd.com/vitamins-supplements/ingredientmono-736-Plantain+BUCKHORN+PLANTAIN.aspx?activeIngredientId=736&activeIngredientName=Plantain+(BUCKHORN+PLANTAIN)&source=2

http://www.webmd.com/vitamins-supplements/ingredientmono-97-Plantain+BLACK+PSYLLIUM.aspx?activeIngredientId=97&activeIngredientName=Plantain+(BLACK+PSYLLIUM)&source=2

Purslane info:

http://www.motherearthliving.com/natural-health/portulaca-oleracea-growing-garden-purslane

http://www.motherearthnews.com/organic-gardening/power-packed-purslane-zmaz05amzsel

http://www.motherearthliving.com/natural-health/edible-weeds-101-health-benefits-of-purslane

https://www.drugs.com/npp/purslane.html

Rosemary info:

http://www.almanac.com/plant/rosemary

http://herbgardening.com/growingrosemary.htm

http://www.heirloom-organics.com/guide/va/guidetogrowingrosemary.html

http://www.gardenersworld.com/how-to/grow-plants/how-to-take-rosemary-cuttings/

http://www.webmd.com/vitamins-supplements/ingredientmono-154-rosemary.aspx?activeIngredientId=154&activeIngredientName=rosemary&source=1

Roseroot info:

http://homeguides.sfgate.com/cultivate-rhodiola-rosea-21776.html

http://www.luontoportti.com/suomi/en/kukkakasvit/roseroot

http://www.phillyvoice.com/herbal-roseroot-fights-depression-upenn-study/

Saffron info:

http://www.saffronbulbs.com/culture.htm

https://www.gardeningknowhow.com/edible/herbs/saffron/growing-saffron-crocus.htm

http://www.vegetablegardener.com/item/2405/how-to-grow-saffron/page/all

https://www.gardeningknowhow.com/edible/herbs/saffron/growing-saffron-indoors.htm

http://www.webmd.com/vitamins-supplements/ingredientmono-844-saffron.aspx?activeIngredientId=844&activeIngredientName=saffron&source=1

Sage info:

http://www.almanac.com/plant/sage

http://herbgardening.com/growingsage.htm

http://www.heirloom-organics.com/guide/va/guidetogrowingsage.html

http://www.totalhealthinstitute.com/health-benefits-sage/

http://www.gardena.com/int/garden-life/garden-magazine/how-to-cut-and-multiply-sage/

http://www.motherearthliving.com/Cooking-Methods/sage-varieties-growing-tips-recipes

http://www.webmd.com/vitamins-supplements/ingredientmono-504-SAGE.aspx?activeIngredientId=504&activeIngredientName=SAGE

Saracen's Consound info:

http://worldofsucculents.com/how-to-grow-and-care-for-senecio/

http://www.complete-herbal.com/culpepper/saracen.htm

https://www.thespruce.com/senecio-plants-1402876

https://www.rhs.org.uk/advice/profile?PID=299

http://www.botanical.com/botanical/mgmh/r/ragwor02.html

https://www.merriam-webster.com/dictionary/Saracen%27s%20comfrey

Saxifrage info:

http://www.telegraph.co.uk/gardening/howtogrow/3309217/How-to-grow-saxifrage.html

https://www.gardeningknowhow.com/ornamental/groundcover/rockfoil/growing-rockfoil-plants.htm

http://plants.for9.net/edible-and-medicinal-plants/pimpinella-saxifraga/

http://www.pfaf.org/user/Plant.aspx?LatinName=Pimpinella+saxifraga

https://www.botanical.com/botanical/mgmh/s/saxbur27.html

http://www.webmd.com/vitamins-supplements/ingredientmono-219-PIMPINELLA.aspx?activeIngredientId=219&activeIngredientName=PIMPINELLA

Self-Heal info:

http://www.motherearthliving.com/Plant-Profile/AN-HERB-TO-KNOW-7

http://www.herbs2000.com/herbs/herbs_self_heal.htm

http://www.gardenershq.com/Prunella-Self-Heal.php

http://www.webmd.com/vitamins-supplements/ingredientmono-130-SELF-HEAL.aspx?activeIngredientId=130&activeIngredientName=SELF-HEAL

Slippery elm info:

https://www.gardeningknowhow.com/ornamental/trees/elm/slippery-elm-information.htm

https://www.na.fs.fed.us/spfo/pubs/silvics_manual/volume_2/ulmus/rubra.htm

https://www.treehelp.com/slippery-elm-seeds/

http://www.umm.edu/health/medical/altmed/herb/slippery-elm/

http://www.herbs2000.com/herbs/herbs_slippery_elm.htm

http://www.webmd.com/vitamins-supplements/ingredientmono-978-slippery+elm.aspx?activeIngredientId=978&activeIngredientName=slippery+elm&source=1

Soapwort info:

http://www.motherearthliving.com/Natural-Health/saponaria-officinalis-growing-soapwort

https://plants.ces.ncsu.edu/plants/all/saponaria-officinalis/

http://www.bhg.com/gardening/plant-dictionary/perennial/soapwort/

http://www.gardenershq.com/Saponaria-Bouncing-Bet.php

http://www.webmd.com/vitamins-supplements/ingredientmono-510-Soapwort+WHITE+SOAPWORT.aspx?activeIngredientId=510&activeIngredientName=Soapwort+(WHITE+SOAPWORT)&source=2

http://www.webmd.com/vitamins-supplements/ingredientmono-25-Soapwort+RED+SOAPWORT.aspx?activeIngredientId=25&activeIngredientName=Soapwort+(RED+SOAPWORT)&source=2

Sorrel info:

http://www.motherearthnews.com/organic-gardening/vegetables/growing-sorrel-zw0z1312zsto

http://www.harvesttotable.com/2009/03/how_to_grow_sorrel/

http://www.heirloom-organics.com/guide/va/guidetogrowingsorrel.html

http://www.webmd.com/vitamins-supplements/ingredientmono-718-SORREL.aspx?activeIngredientId=718&activeIngredientName=SORREL

Sow fennel info:

https://www.shootgardening.co.uk/plant/peucedanum-verticillare

http://www.essexbiodiversity.org.uk/species-and-habitats/trees-and-plants/sea-hogs-fennel

http://davesgarden.com/guides/pf/go/231278

http://www.naturalmedicinalherbs.net/herbs/p/peucedanum-officinale=hog's-fennel.php

http://www.botanical.com/botanical/mgmh/f/fenhog05.html

St. John's Wort info:

https://www.gardeningknowhow.com/edible/herbs/st-johns-wort/st-johns-wort-plant-care.htm

http://www.gardenershq.com/Hypericum-St-johns-wort.php

http://gardenersnet.com/herbs/stjohn.htm

https://www.restorationseeds.com/products/st-johns-wort

https://www.gardeningknowhow.com/edible/herbs/st-johns-wort/st-johns-wort-plant-care.htm

https://www.gardeningknowhow.com/edible/herbs/st-johns-wort/pruning-st-johns-wort.htm

https://umm.edu/health/medical/altmed/herb/st-johns-wort

http://www.webmd.com/vitamins-supplements/ingredientmono-329-st+john+wort.aspx?activeIngredientId=329&activeIngredientName=st+john+wort&source=1

Stoneroot info:

https://www.nps.gov/plants/medicinal/plants/collinsonia_canadensis.htm

http://www.pfaf.org/user/Plant.aspx?LatinName=Collinsonia+canadensis

http://www.herbs2000.com/herbs/herbs_stone_root.htm

http://www.webmd.com/vitamins-supplements/ingredientmono-89-STONE%20ROOT.aspx?activeIngredientId=89&activeIngredientName=STONE%20ROOT

Storksbill info:

http://www.thegardenhelper.com/erodium.html

http://www.gardenershq.com/Erodium-Herons-bill.php

http://www.swcoloradowildflowers.com/Pink%20Enlarged%20Photo%20Pages/erodium%20cicutarium.htm

http://www.herbs2000.com/herbs/herbs_herb_robert.htm

http://www.webmd.com/vitamins-supplements/ingredientmono-24-HERB%20ROBERT.aspx?activeIngredientId=24&activeIngredientName=HERB%20ROBERT

http://montana.plant-life.org/species/erod_cicu.htm

Tansy info:

http://www.gardenersnet.com/flower/tansy.htm

http://www.gardening.cornell.edu/homegardening/scene6aab.html

http://www.webmd.com/vitamins-supplements/ingredientmono-256-tansy.aspx?activeIngredientId=256&activeIngredientName=tansy&source=1

Thyme info:

http://herbgardening.com/growingthyme.htm

http://www.bbc.co.uk/gardening/basics/techniques/propagation_takeherbcuttin gs1.shtml

http://www.almanac.com/plant/thyme

http://www.webmd.com/vitamins-supplements/ingredientmono-823-THYME.aspx?activeIngredientId=823&activeIngredientName=THYME

http://www.medicalnewstoday.com/articles/266016.php

http://www.webmd.com/vitamins-supplements/ingredientmono-702-thyme.aspx?activeIngredientId=702&activeIngredientName=thyme&source=1

Turmeric info:

http://www.gardeningblog.net/how-to-grow/turmeric/

http://www.gardenguides.com/101107-grow-turmeric.html

http://www.globalhealingcenter.com/organic-herbs/growing-turmeric

http://www.webmd.com/diet/supplement-guide-turmeric#1

Valerian info:

http://www.webmd.com/vitamins-supplements/ingredientmono-870-valerian.aspx?activeIngredientId=870&activeIngredientName=valerian&source=1

http://www.heirloom-organics.com/guide/va/guidetogrowingvalerian.html

http://www.fusionperfumery.com/recipes.htm

Vanilla info:

http://www.livestrong.com/article/298410-what-are-the-health-benefits-of-vanilla-extract/

http://www.diethealthclub.com/health-food/vanilla-health-benefits.html

http://www.doityourself.com/stry/how-to-plant-and-grow-vanilla-beans

https://www.gardeningknowhow.com/ornamental/flowers/orchids/grow-vanilla-orchid.htm

Wood Betony info: See Betony

Wood sorrel info:

http://www.gardenershq.com/Oxalis-Shamrock-Sorrel.php

http://homeguides.sfgate.com/grow-wood-sorrel-54450.html

http://www.webmd.com/vitamins-supplements/ingredientmono-228-wood+sorrel.aspx?activeIngredientId=228&activeIngredientName=wood+sorrel&source=1

Wormwood info:

http://www.growing-herbs.com/herbs/wormwood.htm

http://www.gardenershq.com/Artemisia-wormwood-tarragon.php

http://www.webmd.com/vitamins-supplements/ingredientmono-729-WORMWOOD.aspx?activeIngredientId=729&activeIngredientName=WORMWOOD

Yarrow info:

http://umm.edu/health/medical/altmed/herb/yarrow

http://wellnessmama.com/7106/yarrow-herb-profile/

http://usesofherbs.com/yarrow

http://www.hgtv.com/outdoors/flowers-and-plants/flowers/yarrow-uses

http://www.livescience.com/52524-flavonoids.html

http://learningherbs.com/remedies-recipes/natural-insect-repellent/

http://www.gardeningknowhow.com/edible/herbs/yarrow/growing-yarrow.htm

Yawroot info:

http://www.botanical.com/botanical/mgmh/q/queens03.html

https://www.cloverleaffarmherbs.com/queens-delight/

http://www.herbs2000.com/herbs/herbs_queens_delight.htm

Versailles history

http://www.telegraph.co.uk/culture/film/11542992/A-Little-Chaos-who-was-Andre-Le-Notre.html

http://www.worldsiteguides.com/europe/france/gardens-of-versailles/

http://www.britainexpress.com/History/english-gardens.htm

https://en.wikipedia.org/wiki/Gardens_of_Versailles

http://www.classicaladdiction.com/2014/04/the-classical-knot-garden-and-parterre/#.WJs2CtxBSUk

https://en.wikipedia.org/wiki/Bosquet

Made in the USA
Middletown, DE
03 May 2018